CONTENTS

A Century of Cycles 1
   What and When of Life 2
   Your birthchart 3

Age Cycles 5
   Early Years 6
   Steps to Maturity 8
   The Second Chapter 10
   Mid-Life Crisis 12
   Third Act 17
   Personal Cycles 22
   Evolutionary Cycles 22

Years 23

Generations 107
   The Big Picture 108
   Pluto 110
   Neptune 118
   Uranus 124

Cycles of the Century 137

Millennium 143

Glossary 147

For Stephen and Judy with love

Patterns of life and history

Cycles of the planets paint the background of our personal lives. Events used to illustrate their transits merely skim the surface of history and readers may discover even clearer patterns of this century for themselves.

October 1999

A Century of Cycles

How things have changed in a mere hundred years. For better and worse. We behave differently, think differently, travel differently and can view our planet as a small globe floating in space instead of a vast land of unexplored possibilities filled with strange cultures we were unlikely to meet. Now with the flick of a switch internet lands us in the remotest places and carries our gossip from place to place with the speed of light.

The circumscribed lives of our ancestors are hard to compare with our wide choices and hectic pace. Western societies have experienced stark extremes, beginning with the long-skirted fashions of Victorian times to the briefest of modern minis, and from the stately progress of a Model-T to the road rage along the highways of today.

Birthcharts tell two separate stories, a personal one as we develop the energy of our faster planets, and a collective one, seen in the cycles of the slow planets. The patterns of the outer planets are imprinted somewhere in our destiny and will be experienced as a particular strength to share with others or as a phase of history to be be endured.

This book attempts to chart the patterns of recent history as a background to our lives and place in a universal scheme. Individually we are so different and so complicated but are all going the same way on the same spaceship.

In three sections it describes a personal journey through different **ages**; the type of **year** in which we arrived; and the strengths of the **generation** to which we belong. Putting all that together gives the 20th century a progress report and provides good clues about our purpose, and we do have one!

Use the **Age** section to look back and assess the importance of significant years in your life.

The **Year** section is a brief synopsis of the history of your birth year and a description of where you joined an ongoing process.

The **Generation** section links groups together with similar goals, to show the repetition in the planets' cycles. For example, those born in the Twenties, with parents who had survived WWI, grew up to fight in WWII and their children were ripe for Vietnam. The children of the Dirty Thirties suffered the disappointments of the fifties and financial set-backs in the seventies and nineties. The Baby Boomers, offspring of survivors of WWII, turned the world upside down in the sixties and their children grew up in the undisciplined eighties and nineties, still protesting.

So it goes on, and we are making progress even if it is shrouded with chaos.

What and When of Life
(the how, where and why are up to you)

Every individual is part of a universal design that is changing according to a cosmic calendar and the planets provide sign posts and timetables if only we know how to read them. Each of us has our own strengths and weaknesses and a timetable to exercise them, then learn from the inevitable mistakes that occur in every lifetime.

We do have a life of our own, but we also have a loftier purpose, some of which we share with others born around the same time and in the same chapter of history. If you have ever wondered why parents and children seldom understand each other it is because generations have different priorities shown by the changing positions of the slow planets.

The idea that there is a correlation between heaven and earth has been around for a long time. Earlier than 500 BC Pythagoras was teaching that patterns formed by the planets reflect what is happening here on earth — "as above so below" — and believed that freedom for individuals lay in using those patterns to develop spirituality so that souls could overcome the trap of material needs. In the 17th century, Johannes Kepler, mathematician and astrologer/astronomer, was contemplating the mystery of "why am I what I am?" He discovered that our galaxy consisted of symmetrical figures, and calculated that there was a Harmony of the Spheres like a beautiful cosmic symphony, with individuals playing different instruments but the same music.

Astrology helps to understand who we are as individuals and the tunes being played in our lifetime. The fast planets, representing our personal talents, affect us early in life as we establish a physical, emotional and mental Self. Maturing means growing out of the small world of the I and reaching beyond our immediate community to become a member of a global society. Then we can use personal attributes for the advantage of both ourselves and the world.

It is the cycles of the slow planets which lead us into that wider existence. Their positions in a birthchart show the collective lessons we are sharing with others of the same generation, while contemporary events help to illustrate the type of circumstances the soul has come to improve. In other words, the year and the generation of birth define something important that each of us has to contribute to the whole, if spiritual progress is to continue.

The learning cycles occur at definite ages when Saturn is testing maturity and Uranus brings the crises, mid-life and otherwise, to keep us moving ahead. Neptune's disappointments strengthen the reality of faith; and Pluto brings the ultimate test of values. All useful lessons for developing our God-given urge to evolve. As each **cycle** is completed it can bring either a step up to a different level in a **spiral** of understanding, or another trip on the merry-go-round.

At the time of your birth, the planet Earth was having its own experiences as it too develops a collective wisdom. The movements of the planets are mirroring the strengths and weaknesses that could be called the "flavor of the year" as directives for us to understand and use freewill to follow them.

Being born in a difficult era does have its advantages when history repeats similar circumstances. For example, those born in the '30s are equipped to cope well with limited resources. Then the emotional disappointments of the '50s taught a new approach to relationships. And the aggression surrounding the '70s and '80s encouraged those born then to discipline their own anger.

Your birthchart

A birthchart, like a road map, identifies the bumps as well as the hills and valleys of our journey through life. Planets are not doing things to us so much as pointing a direction, and explaining urges and actions, often unconscious, that influence our choices. And we do have choices. It is our range of free-will that sends us off course. A moment of birth is unique, whether it is for an animal, a person, a country or a corporation. Personal experiences are needed to develop the "Me" in each one of us, so that we can become the confident hero of our own soap opera. But we are short-changing ourselves, and our community — be it age-group, country, culture, or tribe — if we think that is enough. Individual purpose and destiny are more complicated and a good deal more satisfying, than just bothering about ourselves. As the world shrinks into a global village human evolution seems to be speeding up and if each wave of souls arriving here learns then teaches something special to benefit the whole of humanity we can all learn faster.

You are a unique individual and will not respond to life's challenges in quite the same way as anyone else because you are starting with a different set of tools. But there are historical situations which you share with others and the year of your birth shows the priorities of human development at that time, and the hurdles that you, and your generation, are particularly well-suited to overcome. Your own birthchart will describe in detail your personality, how you face life and what you are searching for in others to complement your own patterns. It will show you what areas of life are likely to be the ones in which you have your most important experiences. And it will suggest habits and behavior that would make it easy or difficult for you, personally, to tune into your higher purpose.

The next lesson is to deal with whatever you share with groups born around the same time. As you grapple with life's complexities it might be comforting to remember that, simultaneously, there are others who are having the same kind of learning experiences as you, even though the circumstances may seem quite different. The bottom line for everybody is that we are all in this together and our individual performance does make a difference to the operation of the whole, however unlikely that might seem.

At various times in this century events have propelled us around corners, slowly at first but accelerating to a frenetic speed in the last few decades as we seek harmony on earth.

We grow through experiences which occur in cycles as the planets form aspects to each other at various ages. Your year of birth can explain "what" you have come to undergo, digest, then teach the rest of us, and your age can tell you "when" the unconscious part of yourself is ready to focus on getting on with it. Whatever *it* is.

The **Age** section of this book shows which period of life you are in at present, or were in when significant events happened to you. This is a way to consider why you had certain experiences at certain ages and what they taught you about yourself. To make sense of your place in history, you can refer to the **Year** section to check what was happening when you arrived, and the **Generation** section to understand those who came with you. If you bear in mind that you chose to be born into a particular era and set of circumstances the descriptions of the times might help you to understand the team effort you and your peers are here to make. Learning from the mistakes of history made before you came means you can evolve and reach a higher level of wisdom than past generations, instead of continuing on a round-about.

Because planets move at different speeds, and appear to go both forwards and backwards, it is advisable to read the years before and after your birth for a more complete portrayal of your task. .

This book shows how the planets work together to keep us progressing. Checking your personal time table helps to make sense of it all and shows how to proceed in an upward spiral. And that is what life is all about.

AGE CYCLES

Astrology, like numerology and the Tarot, divides life into three separate chapters — or three distinct periods of growth. Each one has its own goal and each goal leads to a higher level of human development, spiraling towards the true potential of an individual.

In the first chapter you are dealing with whatever circumstances you chose to be born into. Perhaps to deal with unfinished business from a former life, or to learn about yourself through your reactions to being controlled by others. It is the period of life in which you seem to have the least freewill since power is not in your hands.

In astrology this is defined by the first cycle of the planet Saturn, which takes from 28 to 30 years to complete. In numerology you are under the first number of the birth path — the month — which represents karma, what has been earned or unfinished in a former life; and in Tarot, the first seven cards of the major arcana represent the "realm of the gods" meaning that you are not in your own world, and not yet in control.

The symbolism for each of these tools suggests that some restrictive authority sets limits for about the first 30 years, until you have learned to take responsibility for whatever unique purpose you have been born. Saturn can seem like a hard task master but it is the hand that guides, and limits, until the timing is right.

The next chapter is the second Saturn cycle, from the age of 30 to about 59. In numerology the Soul number — the day of birth — takes over, and in the Tarot, the next seven cards represent the journey through earthly experience, all illustrating the middle of life when you are building and achieving in your own world. The third chapter is another Saturn cycle, from 59 until the end of life; the year of birth in numerology, the Final Challenge, and the last seven cards of Tarot's major arcana, are for developing spiritually, strengthening the inner world and the Higher level of self, and preparing to withdraw.

A useful timetable for assessing progress is set by the slow planets (Saturn, Uranus, Neptune and Pluto) showing at what ages we reach significant points of crisis. How readily we work with their schedules depends on our freewill but there are certain times in every life when we reach corners that must be turned and check points that help to show how far we have come.

All the planets move in cycles, each cycle having four significant points, similar to the phases of the moon, a beginning (a conjunction, like the new moon) a waxing square (a half moon, a quarter of the cycle) the half-way point (a full moon, half way round the cycle) and the waning square (the final half moon, three-quarters of the circle).

While we are young, a need to abide by other people's rules often contradicts an unconscious urge to be unique. Throughout life two urges, to accept limits (symbolized by Saturn) and to be a free spirit (Uranus), take turns dominating until they find a way to live in harmony and share mutual goals. At certain ages, one or other of these impulses demands attention in ways that can make us seem either rigid or rebellious. Or even both.

Ideally, we mature at the right pace so that we gradually become our own boss without frustrating our evolving purpose. To be willing to take responsibility for our actions and to learn by mistakes is a test of maturity.

There is a joy in aging, in spite of the aches and pains as the body reacts to the wear and tear of time. The spirit and vital life force can continue to flourish with increased wisdom, having the satisfaction of recognizing just how far you have progressed.

Early Years

The unfolding of individuality happens in stages with the first signs of self-expression beginning as early as six months when the ego is ready to separate from mother at the time the Sun is opposing its natal position. How much separation takes place will depend on how strong the Sun is in the chart.

At the age of **seven**, when Saturn moves into its first waxing square (90 degree angle to its natal position) the first crisis of self-assertion has to be faced.

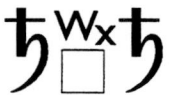

It is time for the young child to emerge from the dependency of babyhood and start being a person in its own right. At seven most normal children become little activists, pushing and fighting for their bit of territory. They have not come here to stay supine creatures who have everything done for them and their need for action is to express the tiny seed of individuality that is making itself felt. The child that is you is getting ready to challenge authority seriously for the first time and this often causes conflict with parents, teachers and other siblings or with anyone you identify as trying to control you. Inner feelings begin to show and emotional and physical growth either quickens or slows down depending on how successful you feel about your first serious attempt to be you.

A waxing square of any planets to their original position is a critical time, offering a choice of taking some personal action and moving forward, or accepting that it is too much trouble and sinking backwards. This is specially important in the case of Saturn, the symbol of maturity. Giving in at this first challenge can hold back the growing-up process until the inner urge to progress reasserts itself.

Between **seven** and **14** the first outside frustrations become evident. A baby in a pram may enjoy being physically confined by a tightly tucked in blanket but not for long. After seven this tender plant of childhood becomes aware of emotional and mental frustrations. The instinct for competition begins to flourish and the will to survive grows stronger. This is a crucial time for persons in authority to stay on guard, without seeming to pressure, but to ward off any blows the child is not ready to withstand. In a childlike way, the individual is learning to function and relate to its surroundings so that it will be ready to face the big tests of cooperating with others around **14**.

At **12** Jupiter, the urge to digest, or at least ingest, more of life physically, emotionally and mentally, is completing its first cycle. Joseph Campbell, the renowned mythologist, believed that humans were born 12 years too soon, unable to fend for themselves! In this first cycle of growth we have learned to walk, talk, and respond to social signals but now new ideas are being born. Wider interests make this age a period of expansion and exploration of the social world a little beyond what has now become familiar territory. Because it is a time of optimism and exaggeration, growth can get out of hand, like a weed. This is when a firm hand is needed to steer a child's developing curiosity and value system in the right direction. Like a first pruning, it needs to be done when the emotional climate is right.

In primitive societies **12** is the age for initiation when the male child has to leave the mother's protection and be introduced to the tougher world of masculine adulthood. Adult guidance at this age, for both girls and boys, sets a pattern for the rest of life. An equal mixture of love and toughness at this time can have a powerfully positive effect on the process of maturing, but if they are not balanced it might take another Jupiter cycle to put things right. Jupiter's 12-year cycles continue throughout life, bringing regular opportunities for expansion of understanding. Around the ages of **24, 36, 48** etc. are appropriate times to check one's progress since the last 12-year mark. These are occasions when a period of mental assimilation can complete one level of understanding so that another bite of life, or step towards wisdom, can be taken. It is a time when subtle and caring criticism can accelerate the processes of learning.

Soon after **14**, when transiting Saturn opposes your natal Saturn, comes a challenge to develop objective awareness, perhaps through another person. The real "Self" in the child is ready to look outside himself, or herself. The ego, like a periscope, is searching for something familiar so that a measurement can be taken of who, what or where you really are. Up to now instinct has dominated but with this opposition the first glimmers of understanding light up the shape of your identity as your own person. Instinct is no longer a blind groping in the dark. By dealing with others of the same age, there comes a dawning that not everyone is the same as you. A new urge to relate and a new level of self-confidence can be reached by testing the limits of authority in a more mature way than was tried by the seven-year old. Instead of challenging someone else, this test is to try working as a partner. The beginning of puberty is, symbolically, a movement towards a new stage of cooperation and should be a time when personality blossoms through interaction with others.

Taking responsibility for yourself is the lesson at this time and, if it is not learned now, there will be either some separation from people upon whom you have relied in the past, or an increase of their control which can act like a frost killing off the early, and vulnerable, flowers of adulthood. The important trials of this age offer a new consciousness of identity as a step towards the next stage.

Steps to Maturity

In our fast-service society we expect instant growth when, in fact, it takes place in shaky steps. Somewhere between an 18th and 19th birthday it is time to expect some emotional experience that is designed to bring a deeper understanding of yourself. It is the end of the first cycle of the Nodes, two points where the paths of the Sun and Moon intersected at your birth. Although there is no heavenly body there to mark the place, symbolically it means that your yin and yang are in contact at that degree of the zodiac and whenever it is activated a fated event could take place helping you to follow your life's purpose. Perhaps a chance meeting with someone who influences you, or makes you see yourself in a different light.

Years ago, a traditional gift given for a 21st birthday was a key to the door as a recognition of new responsibility. Now-a-days young people are expected to grow up earlier, and a doorkey would be more fitting for a 16th or 18th birthday, with the additions of a license to drive and a vote. Physiologically a "child" does not stop growing until after 21, though today, it would be a backward character who did not expect to be fully adult long before that time.

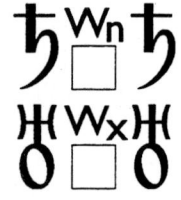

By 21 many young people already have children of their own, starting on a second cycle before they have finished their first. But astrologically, at that age you reach a new stage, when both Saturn (the authority) and Uranus (independence) are at important turning points. Saturn puts us in position of taking responsibility and reminds that it is time to be realistic, and when it is in its waning square (at 21) a crisis is likely to test your ability to behave like an adult. Uranus, known as the Awakener, is the urge that makes us restless and at its first waxing square (at 21) it opens doors to something new, offering an option to go forward or remain stuck in a childhood rut. These two planets are opposing forces within us, acting like red and green traffic lights. As they will be your guides on and off for the rest of life it helps to acknowledge them early, and when they are attracting attention simultaneously (as they are at 21 and will again between 28 and 30) it bodes well to combine caution with change.

Up to this point, parents or teachers have represented the gods in whose world you have been living, and who have influenced your direction. Their views of your potential may, or may not, have helped you to find the path that is right for you. With a waxing square of the planet of individuality and rebellion (Uranus) this is a time to draw distinctions, if there are any, between the different aims of you and your family. But do it with a rational statement of intent, rather than a fight. You should be ready to accept, consciously, that you are outgrowing your early environment and need to begin to pull away from the past to develop your own style, but Saturn expects you to be sensible and take responsibility for the results.

With your inner sense of uniqueness starting to assert itself, there is often a desire to rebel against authority, and that may be a hint that you are still allowing yourself to be dominated by the views of others but are unconsciously ready for change. At this stage, too much rebellion can be destructive. Since the first of your life's chapters will not be complete until the end of your twenties, what is required now is patience and willingness to learn from others. Most people in their twenties think they are ready to take charge, and they could be if they accept that there is still some growing-up to be done. It is an appropriate time to make changes, drastic ones if necessary, but always with the understanding that you are not quite as wise in the ways of the world as you imagine yourself to be. That is a truism that is hard to digest. But you are not out of the karmic woods until after Saturn has finished its first cycle.

From **21** to **28** comes the completion of a process that first became apparent at seven. The breaking away from whatever constitutes the past, tradition, the parental world, now has to take place. The first cycle is coming to an end and unless the second one is going to be a repeat performance, like a spinning disc with the needle stuck, playing the same old theme over and over until it becomes really boring, then there has to be a spurt of new growth. A jump from the circle to the spiral.

The quality of your maturity at the age of 21 can often be measured by the type of parenting you have received in terms of emotional support and guidance. If the childhood urge for security has been balanced with the opportunity to try out your own wings, a sense of being a person in your own right may have been well established by this age. The groundwork has been laid and, if the roots are firm, you are now ready to test out your own theories of what you wish to achieve.

Emotional Needs

In a birthchart, the influence of early homelife is symbolized by the vertical axis, from the point at the base of the chart to the midheaven (known as the MC — medium coeli) at the top. In astrological terms, the personal potential for dealing with security and responsibility is illustrated by the needs of the Moon and Saturn (their aspects, signs and house positions). As life proceeds the progressions of the Moon and the transits of Saturn set a timetable for growing, with the Moon stirring up unconscious emotions and Saturn helping to build a secure structure for any new awareness.

When these two processes are out of sync, there is often a temptation to want the best of two worlds, marriage and childhood, by taking on a partner who is a mother- or father-figure. In that way you can feel that you have a new role and can fill emotional needs without losing the support of someone who represents parental authority, the old security structure. But, as the song says, marriage has to be both the horse and carriage — the Moon and Saturn. Marrying a parent figure is a compromise with reality and a cop-out which is doomed to fail in the long run. Marriage is intended to be a partnership of equal individuals, not a protective cocoon for one or the other.

There is a case to be made for slightly different timing in the assuming of maturity by a male and a female. For a woman ready for child-bearing there can be a temporary advantage to remaining protected if the supportive partner becomes a defense during the vulnerable period of pregnancy, a time when a woman needs plenty of help to grow into parenthood herself. This may mean that equality in the partnership is delayed until the young mother has regained her sense of self in her new role. But eventually equality must come, otherwise the frustration of an unbalanced partnership will set in and fester as time goes on.

Turning **30** is the real step into adulthood, though by that age many of us have laid foundations that are not suitable for the life we want to live. Between 28 and 30 is the time when the walls that have been around since birth finally fall down, or can be removed brick by brick. At last. If there is any ill-feeling locked into a situation which was initiated too early, now is the time to do some restructuring. With a few repairs and a bit of reorganization, the past can be made workable without drastic upheavals. But it is a time for deliberate checking to make sure your foundation is solid. Otherwise, in future years a shaking and shifting will take place, the result of building with sand castles instead of good firm rock.

The Second Chapter

The second chapter is Saturn dumping responsibility right into your lap. Out of kindergarten at last you are ready to put into practice what you have learned. The future is yours to build, within reason and your potential. The years from **28** to **30** are crucial in setting the scene for a brand new chapter. You are leaving the realm of the gods and entering a world in which you can build your own castles. In numerology you are now under the central number of your birth path, the day of birth, a time to shine in your own right. In Tarot the next group of the major arcana is the journey through the "earthly experience" from the cards of Strength (sometimes known as Justice) to Temperance, an opportunity to show what you are made of.

In astrology several important aspects are occurring simultaneously suggesting that a major restructuring of the ego is taking place. It is time to break down old barriers then attempt to rebuild to your personal specifications. Sometime during these two years the Sun and Moon repeat their natal pattern to each other, which means that the progressed Moon has completed its first cycle, and each area of your life has undergone emotional reaction of some kind. Also Saturn returns to its original degree and Uranus, the planet of individuality, is in a comfortable situation (a trine) to its natal position. Saturn is ready to start another 30 years of experience, and the waxing trine of Uranus, known as a second birth, is an invitation for some mental creativity to blossom. It is your opportunity to start forging your own history.

This conglomeration of aspects can bring a crisis on the physical plane when some part of life is out of balance, if such an event is needed to get your conscious attention. For example someone who was an excellent athlete but who was concentrating too much on the physical and neglecting the intellectual side of her character injured her knee and had to sit still for a change. This was Saturn taking charge for her own good so that new knowledge could lead to the development of the other, and Higher, Self, which Uranus represents.

It is a very important stage in defining, or redefining, your identity and accepting the challenge to move away from the crowd and stand alone. Adulthood has finally begun and your life is now ready to take on a new shape as you leave the realm of the gods to build your own world.

Turning Point

The age of **30** seems quite late to start the second chapter in our hurried world, but that is nature's time. The astrological second birth takes you into your own world, unlike the first birth which could have seemed like a haphazard dropping into someone's cradle. By now, through trial and error, some of it painful no doubt, you should have a clear view of what you are and where you want to aim your life. This is the best time to work at knowing yourself in as much detail as possible. You are a person like nobody else on earth. You have your own particular combination of DNA, finger-prints and birthchart, the blue-print of energies describing your potential. Now is the time to face reality. If you were born an onion it is fatuous to try to be a daffodil or, in Hans Andersen's terms, stop being a duck and accept that you are a swan.

Mischievous fate sometimes blinds our start in life making it an obstacle race, forcing us to find a way out of the maze through a series of bumps and bruises. Between **28** and **30** a long apprenticeship is ending. If you are already president of the bank, or most successful in your profession, the news for you is that "you ain't started yet"!

Deciding who you are is not an easy task as it sometimes means recognizing what is missing, or what has not gone well for you up to this point. That is what the rebuilding process is all about. By this age, some faulty foundations may have already been laid and covered with the concrete of social habits, which are difficult to dislodge. But if the foundations are not the right ones for you, now is the time to accept the disruption of a little demolition, because sooner or later they will have to be dug up so that building for the future can rest on firmer ground.

Up until **30** you are dealing with the environment into which you were born. After **30** that has to be left behind and you are free to start rebuilding with your own materials. The first reaction to this new freedom is often negative since there may be some reluctance to admit that you could be on a path that is leading in the wrong direction. At this time, when the Moon, Saturn and Uranus are all active, it is important to examine your unconscious habits (Moon) assess carefully not only what goal (Saturn) you have achieved so far, but whether or not it is what your individuality (Uranus) really wants.

This is a time for a new beginning and opportunities will start to open up if you look for them. Old guidelines, which may have become barriers, are now moveable so that something new can be put in their place. If worn-out habits are not examined and changed now, before **35** a feeling of frustration could be overwhelming, taking its toll, either internally or externally.

Mid-Life Crisis

Our "allotted span" used to be considered as three-score years and ten, and though people are living far longer than that these days, we are supposed to be in control of our own life by the age of **35**, the half-way mark. This is a time for testing emotional maturity and becoming more mentally oriented. If the Self has not accepted its separateness from the influence of authority figures around it, it has not yet grown up, and will still be trying to lean on others to provide its satisfaction.

Sometime after **35** circumstances will cause you to take a good look at yourself, your potential, your aims, your responsibilities and your willingness to accept them without trying to control other people or letting them control you. A little honest self-examination now to reassess your whole approach to life will make it possible to go forward faster and with greater assurance.

By the age of **36** Saturn is again squaring its natal position as it was for the first ego-challenges at age seven. This square requires breaking through any denial about yourself you are holding on to. If we start looking around for someone to blame rather than face our own lack of maturity an inner restlessness is likely to develop.

This age sometimes brings a sense of failure or guilt, but neither is appropriate. It is time to get on with life as it is already long past the age to start being yourself. What is needed is, first, an honest appraisal of how well you are developing your potential, then the courage to make any necessary changes.

Fears and psychological hang-ups — and we all have a few — should have been faced and conquered so that limitations can be accepted as guidelines rather than barriers. Saturn, the planet that controls timing, is in charge. This is a period when old emotional ties may have to be broken so that you can take responsibility for your own feelings.

At the same time friendly Jupiter is completing its third cycle bringing home new understanding, so that personal development can be deepened. Jupiter's role is the urge to grow and by now the kind of growth should be to concentrate on increasing knowledge about Self and the world around. The urge of this planet for "more" is not just to provide extra goodies for material satisfaction, as that leads to greed. Now its search should be mental, for better understanding of life and your place in it.

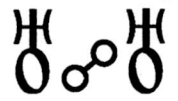

Each generation has new knowledge that will take it one step further into the future than its parents. Uranus, now opposing its natal position, is demanding your attention so that you will be ready to cooperate with the authority that really matters — your own Higher Self. By accepting your individuality and being prepared to stand alone as a unique human being, you should be ready to contribute, in your own special way, to the need for some common global changes. So the Big Four O is delivering you from a childhood world to your global responsibility as an example of a generation. And that is an exciting stepping stone to a completely different scene.

The Big Four 0

Mid-life crises come from the need to adjust to new circumstances and to let go of old patterns that may have been imposed on you by other people and are restricting your personal growth. This is Uranus opposing itself and making sure you, personally, are wide awake to the universal aims of your generation. That kind of self-confrontation and wish to break through any inner tension, usually brings restlessness. At the end of the thirties, if your unconscious sense of individuality feels threatened it may rebel against the present situation just to illustrate its urge for freedom.

Turning **40** can be a traumatic experience but, as the song promises, this is when life begins or, at least, a new attitude to life is due to begin. This is the age — just before or just after 40 — that unconscious forces are making themselves felt, and are ready to break through any conscious resistance with the suddenness and severity of an earthquake.

It is possible to move smoothly from one half of life to the next as long as you already feel independent and are fulfilling your purpose. But if you have not completely broken free from the programming of childhood restrictions, then you are not yet totally out of the eggshell. At this turning point you must be ready to deal with today instead of continuing to live in yesterday otherwise, consciously or unconsciously, you will start to feel dissatisfied.

Emotional ties to the home and family of birth are ready to be replaced by an acceptance of equality with your parents who can now be seen as individuals, no longer responsible for you, or with jurisdiction over your life, except as people to consult because of their wisdom. Now you are dealing with the world on your own terms so that in the second half of life you can achieve your potential as a productive and unique individual.

Your new character may begin to emerge and if it has an unfamiliar face, the first reaction to its appearance can be turbulent with apprehension or impatience, depending on how confident you are. The "new you" can fuel a desire to rebel against anything, or anyone, you feel is holding you back from expressing this newly discovered person.

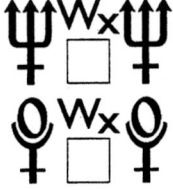
With increasing maturity, the meaning of the outer planets, the slow ones (Uranus, Neptune and Pluto), is due to be tested. New potential is ready to be developed so that living only for oneself is no longer satisfying. If this check point is ignored, when Neptune and Pluto reach waxing squares, around the age of **42**, the need to accommodate yourself to

the new direction could reach crisis level and sudden urges or events will force re-thinking that should have been done a decade earlier. Anyone can suddenly have an urge to be different, to try out dreams that have been set aside for too long, or to follow some intriguing path they have seen at a distance. Individual needs, which have been unrealized until this time, demand to be expressed. If you have been hiding behind a false facade you are about to have a breakthrough, so watch out for strange behavior. Yours.

Partnership Problems

It is no wonder this age is called a time of crisis. People often feel trapped and act erratically from a mood of desperation, sensing that life is passing them by too fast. The Self is challenging itself to continue to grow, and it will not be ignored. Although you may view other people as your jailers, the real opponent is yourself, but this truism takes time to absorb. In the meantime, this can be a disruptive process, specially within a marriage. A partner may be blamed as someone preventing change, or, if the Uranus urge to rebel is being projected on to them, may be seen as the restless force that is upsetting the status quo. One or other partner may begin to break any rules that seem to be too constricting.

In spite of sudden upsets this age brings, it should be looked at as a chance for renewal and a shake-up of whatever part of your life is in danger of stagnating. When a partnership has pockets of strife that have been buried out of habit, or convenience, then some kind of rot can set in that is anathema to healthy growth. So a mid-life crisis is spring-cleaning time for relationships, with a partner, or just with yourself.

From the side-lines, this period could be seen as total self-indulgence but, because we all go through it in some form or other, onlookers need to be patient and forgiving. The Uranus opposition is a period to let off steam, and face the fact that some of our impossible dreams are impossible, or not what we want at all. But we sometimes need time to find that out. About the same time Neptune squares Neptune, focusing on the clearing out of emotional confusion so that insight can take its place. Illusions, or guilt from past mistakes, have to be released, then a little faith that you are here for a spiritual reason can replace them.

After a year or two for any crazy experimentation to work itself out, the individual may want to return to base — if the base is still there — and happily resume the old life with new contentment. This exercise of vaulting over our rainbows is a vital part of maturing. It is a kind of farewell to youth and the lack of realism that goes with it. Being aware of the need to make drastic changes, if they are necessary, rather than holding desperately on to tradition, or security, does make this time more palatable and less destructive.

As long as the second birth occurred smoothly, around **29**, (when Saturn returned) and the adjustments to adulthood were completed in the thirties (before the Uranus opposition) the early forties can be an exciting time. You are about to take a second step towards that objective awareness you started at the age of **14** (when Saturn opposed itself). This is the search for like-minds and mutual support. If they are not found there can be a feeling of loneliness and anxiety. You may be realizing, unconsciously, that you are still on the wrong path. If you are honest with yourself, you can catch up. Then, as you blend your talents with the universal purpose of your generation, the real meaning of partnership becomes obvious and you can get on with whatever it is your were born to do. In other words, when you start to cooperate intellectually in wider spheres than that of your personal life, you will receive encouragement that helps to accelerate your progress.

Facing New Responsibilities

♄ ☍ ♄   By **45**, (when Saturn opposes Saturn) you should be able to accept that your life has a deeper meaning than a personal trip. And that implies that you are ready, willing and able to take new directions as the universe unfolds. The whole of the forties can be testing years and may be difficult for those who resist, or who are not sufficiently mature to accept responsibility for themselves.

These are years of tension if you are pulled one way by growing children and another by aging parents. Feeling trapped by circumstance is hard if you forgot to face your own need for adventure at the end of the thirties and have just worked out a means of exercising some independence, even if it is only independence of thought. You no longer think like your parents, and may be equally antagonistic to the ideas of your teenagers. As the "ham in the sandwich" it is time to accept that each generation is different and that is okay. You have as much right to your beliefs as do the generations either side of you. You are all part of a historical cycle and are contributing in various ways to the evolution of human experience. Knowing that may not diminish the tensions but it does make sense of the balancing act you are in.

♃ ☌ ♃   Around **48** a Jupiter return occurs, beginning its fifth 12-year cycle, which is a period for polishing up your creativity if it is in danger of getting lost in work-related occupations. Presuming you used the fourth cycle to carve out a firm base and cement your material roots this next one is to remember that life has more to offer than just "bread alone". Five is a number associated with joy and Jupiter's optimism can lighten your life up in spite of the obligations that may seem to overwhelm. Its search for meaning needs humor and variety, so developing your originality or finding pleasure in hobbies could offset the seriousness of facing the fifties. The end of the first Jupiter cycle is a move towards adolescence so that the second, between the ages of **12** and **24**, brings experience of partnerships, and the fun of mastering team-work. The next is for increasing the learning curve either with a load of PhDs or good practical experience, whichever is appropriate to your goal. And once you have gained authority in your own right, it is important to catch up with the grown-up child within.

Healing Wounds

Around the age of **50**, with the return of Chiron, which is some kind of inherited scar we are born with, and **51** (with the waning square of Saturn) the challenge becomes one of healing old wounds and finding the Meaning of

Life — no small feat. We are all born with some psychological pain that has to be recognized before it can be healed and Chiron describes it. At the completion of its 50-year cycle, the type of sore spot and how it is working in our life, should be obvious if we want to look for it. Like a sliver it has to be pulled into consciousness and dealt with before it stops bothering us.

The famous astrologer, Dane Rudhyar described the waning square as a crisis of consciousness. If your goals have been too high, or too low, they may be impeding the universal plan laid out for you. Again it is time to be realistic so that diminishing energy is not being wasted. Aging can then be accepted gracefully as a gift of wisdom rather than a loss of youth.

At this age, some attention should be paid to physical needs so that there is no undue strain caused by an unwillingness to give up old habits. People may still want to run the marathon, or play a strenuous game of tennis, and be quite capable of it. But the toll on the body is greater than it was and it is wise to take that fact into account and be prepared to change the future pace accordingly as you age. As at **21**, **50** is time to leave the past behind and look forward to something new and different as the Saturn cycle peaks around **51** bringing its own rewards before it starts to wane with the decade.

In the fifties, you are at the top of your own mountain and the view of your life's purpose should be better than ever. If you survey the scene and strengthen your wisdom by exchanging ideas with others, your experiences will be useful to suggest new methods for dealing with the world's future needs. Take a good look because the time is fast approaching when you will hand over the reins to people coming along behind you. The clearer your mind is now, the more valuable will be the theories you bequeath to others ready to listen to your wisdom.

A really important age is **56**. With Uranus again in trine to its natal position, it is time for a "third birth". This brings the chance to make your most important contribution to the world by putting into practice all that you have learned. Here is the peak opportunity to present ideas born out of your own uniqueness and experience.

If the decision to live on a universal, rather than a personal, level was made back in the forties, relationships should have taken on new meaning. You would have sensed that you were part of a community, and others, who have different skills were allies, and were needed to supply additional dimensions to your own efforts. The fact that "we are all in this together" should have become obvious. But, at that time the drive to succeed rather than to share may have still been your priority. If that was the case, personal relationships may need some serious reconciling at this stage of life. It has been said that a marriage that is happy with its small children will have to do a lot of adjusting when they leave home. And one that is strained while the children grow can be happily revived when they are gone. The late fifties are the years to work at your role as a partner if you want to forge a satisfactory companionship for old age.

Third Act

Between **58** and **60**, you take a major step along the path to the future. You are entering a period when things begin to come together and you can really understand the true meaning of your personal journey. Although full understanding may take some time, there is still plenty of opportunity to ice the cake, so to speak, by making amends where necessary, patching the weak spots and adding some elegant finishing touches to what have been your efforts to build your own world.

For the first time since birth, the planets representing your wish to grow (Jupiter) and the discipline of good timing (Saturn), are both back in their original positions. Jupiter is completing its fifth cycle, prompting a review of your philosophy. And a new cycle of responsibility begins with a second Saturn return (the first having occurred between **28** and **30**). The combination of new Jupiter and Saturn cycles starts a withdrawing process to complete your story and the role you have played as part of a collective consciousness. This is what the ancient Greeks called the Golden Age, a very special time, and, back then, not many people lived long enough to enjoy it. It is the third and final, chapter of life, even if you live to be 110 because you are now in the spiritual part of your trip which will take you gently into the next phase, whatever it is, after death. To give it true meaning turning 60 needs to be faced as a starting point rather than an ending, and an opportunity to make sense of it all.

Jupiter and Saturn are the two urges which guide our social involvement and remind us that "no man is an island". If they work well together they offer opportunities to expand our horizons without getting lost. Jupiter's first round (age **12**) answered the personal need of youth for peer acceptance), and subsequent 12-year cycles mark steps in our growing self-understanding. Then from **30** onwards (after Saturn's first cycle) we were shouldering new kinds of responsibility ourselves while trying to build on our own dreams. As we mature, the Jupiter cycles should add understanding of how the world works, then new wisdom can translate into taking a serious role in our community.

Now that these two planets are beginning new cycles, provided we have paid our dues, it is a second chance to balance responsibility with personal satisfaction, giving and receiving with intelligence. It is a time for cleaning the board ready to move forward again while realizing that there has to be some control (Saturn) on the expanding we want to do (Jupiter). A little middle-age spread is acceptable as long as it is accompanied by a few self-imposed limits.

While searching for new meaning and becoming wise in the ways of the world, it is now possible to fulfill obligations that are supportive of others but not to the extent of feeling fettered. Decisions about responsibility are crucial at this age so that liabilities can be settled or, at least, reduced to manageable proportions. As this part of life's journey begins it helps to lighten the load by restructuring attitudes and shrugging off past mistakes, recognizing them as useful experiences. Then you will no longer be hampered by the weight of regrets or disappointments.

The next step is to accept that your position as an authority is about to change once more. You will soon need to leave room for those starting out on their second chapter (at the age of **28** to **30**), handing over the limelight to younger people and bowing gracefully out of some old responsibilities. Your approach to living can take on new creativity while you move into a more spiritual realm. This time is defined by the year of birth — the Final Challenge — in numerology, and the last seven cards of the Tarot, bringing experience full circle.

Obvious Patterns

Having completed two chapters yourself, you are now in an excellent position to see the pattern of your life cycles. Taking time to recall the circumstances of your own experiences 30 years earlier, (at the time of your first Saturn return) will help to make clear what your individual purpose has been, and will continue to be, with added maturity. By finding some similarity between then and now, you can check your progress and make sure that, if you did not learn something the first time around, you are ready to learn it right now. It is never too late and examining the past can assist the process. Any situation that made you feel frustrated or fearful around the end of your **20s** defines the limits of Saturn. It might have been a person in authority who seemed to be limiting your actions; or an intellectual or emotional barrier that was causing you to hold back, or be held back, at that first Saturn return. Is it still a factor or are you now free from that hemmed-in feeling? Since then you have reached this age of understanding when reality can be accepted cheerfully, and objectively.

The hero of your story — who is you — is getting ready to rest on his, or her, laurels, personal and collective but there should be one more check before you do. As a representative of a particular generation which had its own strengths and weaknesses, and its own historical background, you are now in a position to make a contribution to human evolution by acting as a link between the past and the future. A useful exercise would be to consider the views of others in your age group and size up the abilities and attitudes that made them (and you) different from their parents and their children. In that way you can isolate the specialness of the years surrounding your birth and ask yourself what the world was needing at that time and how well you and your peers filled that need. Were your efforts beneficial or not, if not why not? Once you have assessed the influence of your generation you can understand that you have had a role in making some radical changes.

Age Cycles

From now on, achievement need not, and should not, be a matter of competition. The race for the top is no longer important. Being prepared to move aside in the next few years will allow others to take the lead. Handing over the reins of authority will leave you free to start an inner journey which goes deeper than ever before and will bring you to a point where you can be at peace with yourself and the world. The going will become less strenuous as your direction becomes spiritual rather than material.

By **63**, everyone who is using their individuality positively should feel content to be different and willing to accept the aloneness that comes with that knowledge. Although you are still a member, and hopefully an active one, of the universal society, you can enjoy being a person with unique experiences. No other person can know you totally, or understand all the hopes and hurts, the mistakes and triumphs, that your life has been. And no one is exactly like you. Uranus (now forming a waning square to its natal position) is testing your willingness to be realistic about yourself. And with that strength of mind, the age of **66** (Saturn's waxing square) offers yet another opportunity to be self-assertive, this time using spiritual, rather than physical energy to aim towards a more creative and intangible goal than you sought around the age of **36**, the last time this square occurred.

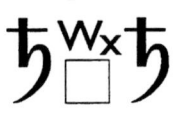

Balancing Act

Any waxing square offers the chance to go forward and if it is not taken then you may slip backwards. At this stage of life this particular square will show how the balancing act between Saturn and Jupiter, started at the beginning of your sixties, is working. A few aches and pains are to be expected but your attitude to them is what will count. If you are not yet comfortable with yourself, unconsciously you will start signaling that you have given up on life but as long as you maintain the open-mindedness and optimism of Jupiter, the rigidity of Saturn will not crystallize into old age too fast. It would be a pity to give up now since there is still plenty to be added to your experiences. Jupiter's urge to grow will continue to keep your interests alive and Saturn's square is an invitation to take action. When people retire, if they have lost the reason for living, some take the easy way out and just close up instead of finding new interests. And that is a waste as there is still so much to learn.

The mid **70s** confirm the wisdom that sharing responsibilities eases the load. For a third time, a Saturn opposition offers a new structure for cooperation, by **73** or **74**. This can be a time of satisfaction for those who have interests outside their personal lives, but for anyone living within a small world, the fear that sooner or later you just might be dependent starts creeping into your consciousness. This opposition need not be about dependence or independence but about finding a practical way to form a sensible relationship with others in the same position as yourself. Ideally, it is a chance to solve problems of aging before you come to the point of having to lean on your children or younger people. Planning ahead means that when that time comes it need not be all taking without any giving. When physical limitations pin you down that is when inner development takes on its true value. With an overall view, you can still be part of the world without insisting on being at the center, as long as you have kept up some interests. How well your spiritual and mental capacities have developed is now crucial to your well-being.

Telling the Story

Watching the future unfold, it will be possible to recognize the influence that your generation has had on recent circumstances. You are part of history and can play a fascinating role in bringing the past to life for younger people with "I was there..." stories. They may not know it but later generations do need your perspective on today to give them a realistic view of their own times. So at **75** onwards, an age when many people feel that the world has left them behind, there is a very useful contribution to be made as a personal historian. This new role calls for the kind of confidence that comes from inner strength such as knowing that you matter without trying to impose your ideas on others, and being peaceful without being too passive.

When peers and friends begin graduating to another realm the fact of approaching mortality cannot be ignored. Energy, physical, mental and emotional is at a premium and this is an age to simplify your life and clear away the clutter invested in belongings. Sorting through the piles of "things" life has collected, and memories that are disturbing, saves lots of energy, then by handing on whatever can be useful to others you have a personal recycling scheme.

The age of **80** is again a time for assessing. With the waning square of Saturn there are new realities to face consciously, as there were at **21** and **51**. It is an important corner to turn in accepting what has been, and sifting through  the triumphs and the errors so that false hopes can be put aside with dignity. The period approaching is similar to the time a gardener checks the successes and failures of last season and starts leafing through seed catalogues to decide what can be done differently when the next planting comes due. There is always another cycle of life to anticipate, even if you are not going to live through it all yourself, on this planet at least. And **80** is the ideal age to look back with discrimination and admit what may have been mistakes, then realize how much you learned from them. This can be the height of your wisdom and if you have kept good communication lines to younger generations they have plenty to learn from you. It is the one time in life that you could write a useful autobiography!

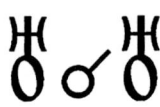 By **84**, Uranus returns to its natal position, completing a personal cycle and, for many of you another one is ready to start, particularly in this time of increasing longevity. This can bring quite a sudden change of thinking as well as a willingness

to adjust to, or at least accept, changes which were resisted during your **70s**. Yet another new birth is approaching bringing more revelations about the meaning of life to those who have retained interests in the world. It is not possible to remain up-to-date when the brain's "floppy discs" get overloaded and the names of the new heroes, film and sports stars, no longer ring a bell! That is okay, we cannot know everything and it is time to be selective. But they are still full of useful information, and when some memories slide away others grow stronger. As long as the mind and the heart are operating you are able to contribute in some way to those around. But prolonging life with machines which enslave the body and mind is a poor substitute for living. It is only postponing a graduation to a higher level of understanding and learning, which is waiting to receive us.

We can continue to learn and to add to life's worth right to the end. New situations can make final answers much clearer. And that is our ultimate wisdom.

Personal Cycles

7............ waxing square of Saturn
12.......... new cycle of Jupiter
14.......... Saturn opposite Saturn
19.......... new cycle of the Nodes
21.......... waning square of Saturn
             waxing square of Uranus
24.......... third Jupiter cycle begins
28-30..... second Saturn cycle begins
             waxing trine of Uranus
             Moon conjunct Moon
36.......... waxing square of Saturn
             fourth Jupiter cycle begins
38.......... third cycle of Nodes begins
38-42..... Uranus opposite Uranus
40-42..... waxing square of Neptune
45.......... Saturn opposite Saturn
48.......... fifth Jupiter cycle begins
50.......... new cycle of Chiron begins
51.......... waning square of Saturn
56.......... waning trine of Uranus
59-60..... third Saturn cycle begins
             sixth Jupiter cycle begins
63.......... waning square of Uranus
66.......... waxing square of Saturn
71.......... seventh Jupiter cycle begins
73.......... Saturn opposite Saturn
80.......... waning square of Saturn
83.......... ninth Jupiter cycle begins
84.......... second cycle of Uranus begins

Evolutionary Cycles *(approx.)*

1891 ... Neptune conjunct Pluto
         (every 490-500 years)
1914 ... Saturn conjunct Pluto
         (every 33 years)
1917 ... Saturn conjunct Neptune
         (every 36 years)
1941 ... Chiron conjunct Pluto
         (every 59 years)
1942 ... Saturn conjunct Uranus
         (every 45 years)
1947 ... Saturn conjunct Pluto
         (every 33 years)
1952 ... Saturn conjunct Neptune
         (every 36 years)
1965 ... Uranus conjunct Pluto
         (every 115-127 years)
1966 ... Saturn conjunct Chiron
         (every 147 years)
1982 ... Saturn conjunct Pluto
         (every 33 years)
1988 ... Saturn conjunct Uranus
         (every 45 years)
1989 ... Saturn conjunct Neptune
         (every 36 years)
1993 ... Uranus conjunct Neptune
         (every 172 years)
2000 ... Chiron conjunct Pluto
         (every 59 years)

YEARS

As history unfolds in its own way every year has a character cast by the planets performing their intricate dances with each other. Humanity reacts unconsciously to the tensions or freedoms of their combinations, sometimes urgent, sometimes relaxed.

We are born into a particular set of patterns that assist or hamper our lessons but being part of a mass movement it is interesting to see how we have dealt individually with the collective hurdles or helpers that our times have supplied. Chaotic though life often seems there is a direction, and progress, as human beings slowly learn from experiences, far too slowly for our life span, but nevertheless in progressive steps.

History certainly colors our personal lives, whether we appreciate that or not, and being dropped into the middle of great cycles of evolution gives us only a small part to play in the whole. But having a walk-on role is important and it is fascinating to look back and see how the drama was progressing at the time of our arrival.

In these critical and uncomfortable years we live in, it could be comforting to realize that we are in a period of "dark before the light" and that there is a healthy side to having agonies and injustices visible instead of moldering underground. If we see them we can do something about them. Can't we? In these times of instant communication we have a responsibility to be informed so that we can have an intelligent opinion. Ignorance is no longer bliss.

The patterns of the slow moving planets, Saturn, Uranus, Neptune and Pluto, and the North Node and Chiron, suggest your role in the collective exercise of improving the world. But your personality and character are defined by the positions of the fast-moving ones, and the angles, at your birth. Of course, personal circumstances and how you respond to difficulties make all the difference to life's satisfaction. If we think of living as an exciting and challenging obstacle race that encourages us to evolve personally and collectively, then identifying the opportunities and trials, and even the timing of major lessons, can be helpful.

The purpose of these brief, and very generalized, explanations of what was going in your year is to offer a background view of the generational chore imprinted on your psyche. They are illustrated, often subtly, by historical events or attitudes of that time. The symbolism of some years is much clearer than for others, depending on how precise were the aspects of the planets.

As well as considering your personal year the overall message of the slow planets at that time helps to define the purpose of your generation in dealing with the transforming energy of Pluto, the spiritual urge of Neptune and the desire for independence of Uranus as human nature matures to a higher level of self-awareness. Since planets move at varying speeds, and do not respect our calendar, the effects of your year of birth may spill over into the one before or the one after and be part of trend which takes years to show.

Inevitably the interpretation of events describing the social and political climate of any year becomes personal, relying as it does for everyone on experience and inclination. The meanings suggested here are ideas to stimulate your own view, which might be quite different.

The likely effects of the hard aspects are also open to question but are useful timetables for progress. They too rely on how a person responds. But a positive approach does help. In this book squares, specially waxing ones, are viewed as encouragement to act in a way that moves one off base, while the waning ones show that it is time to be realistic. The oppositions can be a means of solving blocks and easing tensions whether internal or external. Working out the meanings for yourself can, at least, be enlightening. So enjoy!

1927

This was at year of awakening and an interesting starting point for an acceleration of consciousness that would develop throughout the rest of the century. The spirit of independence and personal freedom was rising as Uranus moved into the first sign of the zodiac, Aries. The "let me out of here" feeling may have led to outright rebellion or an escape into fantasy, or even both. Those urges are symbolized by the flight of Lindberg — first man to cross the Atlantic solo — and the establishment of Hollywood through the formation of the Academy of Motion Pictures.

Every 14 years or so, Jupiter and Uranus meet, as they did this year completing a cycle begun in 1914 which was the prologue to brand new attitudes. Their conjunction suggests it is time to make social (Jupiter) changes (Uranus), and expand knowledge, and, as the last one was in Aquarius, it heralded a surge of rebellion against the old rules. This new one, in Aries, adds enterprise and momentum to the urge to grow. In this case the changes could have been adventurous or selfish, but for those of you born now the need to be recognized as an individual is strong. You are pioneers.

One side of Aries is idealistic and some of your innovations would be to help humanity as a whole. Another side can be too self-involved. Whether you like it or not, you were all born into a class of movers and shakers willing to take risky steps towards introducing new thinking. If Aries is strong in your chart you may act without realizing that other people would follow, and probably prefer to get going alone rather than wait for any plan. Like the Fool of the tarot, or the young knights of myths, you were destined to experience many ups and downs, in the adventure of getting to know yourself.

With four of the five slowest planets (Jupiter, Saturn, Uranus and Neptune) in fire signs for much of the year, you were born into an enthusiastic and optimistic time of "the sky's the limit". But too much enthusiasm can get out of hand. Remember what happened to the stock market two years later when that optimism had turned to greed.

As well as being an evolutionary start this was also a year of dramatic disasters, almost as if nature was making the point, rather forcibly, that it was time for serious changes. There were avalanches, tidal waves, earthquakes, explosions, student riots — something to awaken even the deepest sleepers from their fantasies. Another of nature's ferocious years occurred in 1989 when Uranus was entering Capricorn making its final square to its 1927 position, as a reminder to face reality. More wake-up calls came with devastating oil spills, hurricanes, earthquakes, student demos in Czechoslovakia and Tiananmen Square, the fall of the Berlin Wall and a crash on the Japanese stock market.

In your personal life whatever happened around the years of your two Saturn returns, 1956-57 and 1986, should show how you played the hand you were dealt. Looking back you may see they were times to slow down and reassess. If those dates mean nothing then look again, this time from 1996-98, when Saturn joined your Uranus, then Pluto moved over your Saturn. That was a time for new wisdom curtailing any excessive hopes or fears that had carried you too far from reality. Saturn helps to focus your ideas or at least to limit the search for your personal Holy Grail. Being born in such an exciting year you had, and still have, lots of new horizons.

1928

This was a year for adjusting dreams and narrowing interests to include reality after Neptune moved into the sensible sign of Virgo in August. There was still too much happy-go-lucky escapism about in spite of clues that many balloons were about to pop. The fantasies should have ended two years ago, when Uranus was inconjunct Neptune, but did not. So the first clue to your universal purpose is a Sagittarian one — keep searching for social improvement but beware of Great Expectations. Saturn in the sign of Sagittarius means you cannot believe everything you are told, but when you do change your mind there is no need to "throw the baby out with the bath-water". In other words, rather than believing all is right or all is wrong, try moderation.

Where there has been too much optimism with too little meaning there may have been a bump in your road which brought you down to earth. By the end of the year, an uncomfortable inconjunct aspect forming between Saturn and Pluto was warning that out-of-control optimism would be reigned in sooner or later. Also a self-indulgent trend, of Saturn conjunct the South Node, was narrowing interests everywhere. The message here is that pioneering often requires a "softly, softly" approach rather than a direct face-off. But that is a matter for your discrimination, which is what inconjuncts demand.

When that aspect was joined by Uranus at its midpoint in November, the promise of something sudden and frightening was building up. This was repeated late in 1929. Any questions?

The US was turning towards isolationism as the nation backed away from international involvement. With the exciting mix of a strong Neptune in Leo and Uranus and Saturn also in fire signs there was a great temptation at this time and for those born this year, to concentrate on self and say "I did it my way". (Frank Sinatra was a Sagittarius!) In the long run that is not what your search for perfection is about. The Uranus urge to pioneer is to move into a new age where networking and community are the tools to solve problems. You cannot do everything by yourself.

Your first Saturn return, 1957-58, came with the first signs of space-age competition and increasing civil unrest, two examples of confrontation likely to get out-of-hand. The Soviets launched the satellite, Sputnik, beating the US space program, and colored students faced mobs and police dogs at Little Rock. Both events led, eventually, to big changes but before then illusions about easy progress would be shattered. They were again in 1986-87, your second Saturn return, with the destruction of the Challenger spacecraft and Chernobyl nuclear plant. Two steps forward and one back is a pace to expect.

If taking chances went with your personality, you have probably needed to do a lot of "nettle grasping" during your life-time to get back to reality. But where you have had an over-cautious approach, and ignored an inner rebellion too much tension could have built up. You were born with earthquake tendencies, tuned to social upheavals, and that is exciting providing it is not too destructive. Any desire to gamble was increased around 1971, with Jupiter and Neptune meeting in Sagittarius. Was it fun? Adjusting your sense of adventure to common sense, without squashing either has been your path.

1929

The negative associations with this year need not upset you if their lesson has been absorbed. The planet of expansion, Jupiter, had moved into materialistic Taurus last year, triggering the "gimme more" syndrome, and Chiron, not yet discovered but still marking a psychic wound, was also there. Now sensible Saturn, about to enter the karmic sign of Capricorn, and Neptune moving from confident Leo to doubtful Virgo, with its practical disappointments, were heralding an emotional period of discrimination. Taken together, the planets were signaling that it was time to come down to earth and pay your dues. For many the disastrous financial crash of the year did just that, resulting in a bleak future and world wide shortages. Warnings there last year were largely ignored, and that should remind you to view optimism skeptically and look ahead with lots of common sense.

The long, long cycle of Neptune and Pluto was to close its first semi-square at the end of the year, a hint of coming tensions. It will continue to produce intense emotions of hopes and set-backs until we learn to respect and share, spiritual and material wealth but that could take much longer than any normal lifetime. Those of you born with Jupiter in Taurus and Saturn in Sagittarius have a role in reminding others to respect the Earth and look for the silver lining when things get tense. Any losses associated with Neptune, and there are usually a few, need not be painful if they are seen as clearing away the dross that has been left over from the wrecking crew of Uranus and Pluto which effect us all from time to time. Someone has to tidy up. And the god of the sea was starting a tidal wave of depression that would last a decade. That gave you a sixth sense when trouble is ahead, something your peers born during the last two years are likely to ignore.

For those of you born while Neptune was at the end of Leo (and this includes many 1928 babies), 1994 began an interesting phase. Pluto squared your Neptune, at the same time as Saturn was opposing it, there should, or could, have been an useful dose of reality that helped reform your dreams and showed you how to dig them out of any holes they had fallen into. Around 1983-4, as you were preparing for your "third birth" of Uranus trining Uranus, as happens to everyone in their mid-fifties, Neptune was joining your Saturn warning you to stay alert. In that period of rising apprehensions a record number of people were killed or injured by international terrorists and the "greatest ever" panic buying occurred on Wall Street. How was that for a reminder? As long as you did not succumb to depression yourself, you had something sensible to bring to the table, learned from living through anxiety and coming out the other side.

Your year was definitely a lesson of "what goes up must come down", which means balancing optimism and pessimism. Another balance you can understand comes through being ready to "give and take", sharing the goodies unselfishly to meet unexpected needs. That is something that needed consideration in 1998 when Saturn going into Taurus, limited Earth's bounty. Economic and physical uncertainties like the Bre X mine scandal or El Nino were evidence that something is out of sync. May be the poles have shifted and we are riding a see-saw, but at least you are used to it.

1930

This was a dangerous, but an exciting time to be born. Following the shock of last year's crash, it was a crucial turning point for reviewing the value of material resources. With the North Node and Chiron, (which would not be discovered until 1977) both in Taurus, it was time to respect nature and protect planet Earth. The world was ready for a test of power-sharing, and would learn it through the ever-widening gaps between the haves and have-nots.

A difficult decade started with some severe shocks when many who had felt their future was secure suffered sudden losses. It was a special opportunity to be realistic, and break the cycles of booms and busts caused by financial tensions. Saturn in Capricorn was holding on to archaic rules while Uranus in Aries was rarin' to try something new. This time Saturn won, so the status quo remained dominant. It would take at least another 60 years (until Saturn and Uranus were together in Capricorn) before there was enough social awareness to recognize the dangers of extremes. Lack of family security produced many frightened parents who were either too rigid (Saturn) or too smothering (Pluto in Cancer). Understandable though that may have seemed at the time it was perpetuating Saturn's fears and denying Uranus its chance to experiment. Your task has been to reconsider the dangers of allowing rigid structures to retard progress.

The cycle of Neptune and Pluto, started in 1892-3, moved forward a notch this year when Pluto, the most distant planet yet identified, was actually seen when they were making their first semi-square. Two appropriate events that were tests of mysterious powers took place this year. Then the airship R101 exploded on its maiden flight. And a public seance of thousands of people was held in London after Arthur Conan Doyle's (author of Sherlock Holmes) death. Conan Doyle was a great believer in the after-life and was said to reappear in spirit that night.

Pluto's existence had been assumed since 1912 when it was in Gemini, but nobody had found it until now. At last its meaning could seep into human consciousness. Pluto brings forces of corruption and destruction to the surface so that the need for transformation has to be faced. It also sows seeds for a more fruitful future. Among other things, Pluto represents fortunes, the wealth that brings plutocracy, putting too much power in too few hands. With Saturn in the opposite sign and Uranus at their mid-point, as it had been since November 1928, a struggle for control was underway. It was time to recognize that there was more to life than money if only we could break free of the old system. This was only the beginning of a long lesson about conspicuous consumption and greed as opposed to nature's generosity. There would have to be more wars and panics before exploiters would let go, but being born now helps you to understand the problems.

Largely unnoticed, powerful forces were gearing up as the world entered a period of economic manipulation that would lead to another world war and continuing unrest over supplies of natural resources. Economic ups and downs would test our values for the rest of the century. Within a few years, the destructive force of power was personified by the atom bomb. A growing threat of violence will disrupt societies everywhere until imbalances are confronted and Pluto energy turns to healing.

Your key to personal harmony lies in rooting out a fear of loss left over from the '30s. Any tensions you felt in 1944-45, when Saturn opposing your Saturn squared Neptune and challenged your Uranus, could explain that. Then think back to 1989 for contradictions between your instincts to hoard or let go. Being able to appreciate frugality you can encourage social harmony by limiting possessions and showing how to "live lightly off the land".

1931

Last year's tensions were mild compared to what was happening this year. A compulsive resistance to change was bringing domination and control out front with the "big stick" of poverty and hunger much in evidence. Once again Saturn squared Uranus, as last year, and this time Pluto and Jupiter entered the pattern adding emotional pain conjoining each other and opposing Saturn. More than ever, breaking through such tension requires a calm and cooperative approach.

This was a year of misery for many as the extremes between the powerless and powerful grew. In the Soviet Union Stalin was controlling food deliberately starving his own people while selling grain abroad. In desperation people banded together in mass movements resulting in authorities using harsh measures to maintain control. The jobless rate rose in Europe and the US causing riots in London, hunger marches in Washington and violent strikes in the States and Canada.

Four planets, Jupiter, Saturn, Uranus and Pluto formed a T-square, a pattern of conflict that forces action. If this was your year of birth, note the warning about rigidity in last year's description of parents because the compulsion to control is strong in your psyche too and you would not want to pass it on to your children, surely? What was missing, and what you needed to cultivate, was the kind of cooperation that gives others freedom to be themselves. If you have experienced a lack of team work in your life, this aspect could explain it. In 1960 at your first Saturn return Jupiter was joining it in Capricorn perhaps offering opportunities to grow wiser while Pluto with your Neptune was ready to bring any feelings of victimization to the surface. Then again in 1990, Saturn had its second opportunity to identify problems dealing with control. From 1989 when Neptune reached your Saturn followed by Uranus, it helped to loosen up any defensiveness around you and change attitudes in those close by.

In the meantime power centers were shifting. Symbols noting the change of domination from one side of the Atlantic to the other, were the opening of the Empire State building, highest in the world, in New York, and the British Empire changing to a Commonwealth. It was also the year Japan invaded Manchuria beginning an oriental competition. By 1945 Saturn had moved to your Pluto, as the karmic payment of 1931 debts and Japan suffered a harsh defeat, a reminder that what goes out eventually comes back.

Yours was also a year when the 450-year cycle came under its first tough test when Neptune moved to an angle of 45 degrees from Pluto. The negative side of Pluto represents the many forms of cruelty that exist, and this semi-square was a manifestation of the control a few had over the well-being of many. Neptune in Virgo, was symbolizing the anxiety and suffering of workers who were losing jobs and facing poverty and famines caused by droughts around the world. From the '50s to the late '80s, while the two planets were forming a sextile, solving these problems permanently should have been attempted, before they got worse. But unemployment was still a crisis at the end of the century. Most people in the world are vulnerable to some form of enslavement through income and job and, as the economic strings were being pulled tighter, there was more awareness that the puppets felt powerless to get free. Your purpose involves breaking the old mold of enforced submissiveness and keeping the world's goodies circulating

1932

Having a backdrop of depression and famine for your year of birth cannot be exactly comforting but with all the outer planets in difficult (hard) aspects there must be a lot of energy somewhere in your blueprint that encourages you to break through problems. Rather than sitting meekly with folded hands you can take action and avert a repeat of the slow disintegration of peace that took place through the remains of the '30s decade. The victorious countries of WWI failed to appreciate that losers needed help so problems were exacerbated because of a lack of interest in the misfortunes of others. Take note.

Jupiter opposed Saturn this year, bringing a culmination of a social cycle that started in 1921. Any opposition has a positive side as it is an invitation to work with, rather than against, someone, and since the cycle started in Virgo it concerned work and productivity. It would be surprising if, in your life, you have not had to deal with an occasional disappointment in the work you chose. Such a set-back could encourage you to find new solutions to old problems, if you look for them.

Broken dreams, and there were many this year, can be repaired if the timing and the method are right. Mistakes of the last hundred years were being reaped while Uranus, in a cycle with Pluto started around 1830s, was in its waning square. Old structures needed to be removed and replaced and in your lifetime you are likely to experience a lot of extreme opposition to social changes which have to be made. Fortunately you have enough determination to help bring them about. Like a dispute over a garden fence between suspicious neighbors it is best to develop some far-seeing cooperation and precise projects that will benefit both sides and prevent antagonism. Eventually Pluto in Cancer destroys any plans that are not based on real security for all.

One task for those born during the Depression could be to use your empathy to change certain attitudes. An unfortunate theory that was developing this year was repeated 60 years later when you would have authority to protest it. This was the assumption that those out of work, specially the youth, were too lazy to look for jobs. When people who are in the "haves" category talk of "welfare bums" it may stem from ignorance, but within your psyche there is an understanding of the toll that unemployment takes on one's character.

There were plenty of dramatic events this year, most of them unpleasant which is a hint that you have the means and the responsibility to turn negative forces around. This was the year many banks closed, Lindberg's baby was kidnapped, and a French president was assassinated. In the German government Nazis gained a majority. Thousands of war veterans unable to find work, set up camp in Washington, D.C. On the positive side, a new president, Franklin Delano Roosevelt, who was sympathetic to the powerless was about to present a New Deal, a program which saved many from starvation and the indignity of having nothing to do. And a World Disarmament Conference formed the League of Nations. That did not last long, but at least it was an attempt at international cooperation and a forerunner of the United Nations.

In 1985, Pluto squaring your Saturn in fixed signs, added energy to your determination and could have brought events to push you out of ruts, if you were in any.

1933

This was a challenging pattern to be born into with Saturn inconjunct Neptune and many of you would either decide to push forward determinedly or withdraw because of anxiety. Something in between would be more appropriate. A great slogan for your lifetime has been the rallying cry of the new American president, Franklin Delano Roosevelt, "the only thing to fear is fear itself." It was a year when the designs of power were becoming visible to anyone who could put the pieces of jig-saw together. The independent planet, Uranus, was squaring Pluto showing where the control center lay and what action was needed to break its hold. Neptune was still semi-square to Pluto, an aspect bringing tensions that build into conflict if left unresolved. Drastic action was needed to settle the obvious conflicts between the plutocrats, despots and the rest of us. International financiers were making overt moves with their economic manipulation, holding a first World Petroleum Congress and an Economic Conference of Banks, and selling arms to all sides. Meanwhile dictators were preparing the ground for world domination.

If you need evidence about how to dealt with the difficult aspects of this year, and there were several, remember your experiences of 1962-63, the time of your Saturn return when Pluto was blasting away at your Neptune, perhaps digging deeply into what you feared most. If answers to your personal problems were not clear by then, try 1992, a second Saturn return. By the late '90s, when Pluto squared your Neptune, you will be in a more optimistic position to make good on any mistakes made out of fear.

This year saw the economy hitting bottom and banks going out of business. As soon as FDR, an Aquarian, was inaugurated he took drastic actions. Declaring a Bank Holiday, and shutting them down for four days to stop any panic run on cash, he then took the dollar off the gold standard. To encourage optimism he ended prohibition and started his "fireside chats". His New Deal offered employment which saved many from starvation. Europe was not so fortunate as famine spread in the USSR caused by Stalin's ruthless agenda, and through Germany. Hitler became Chancellor and a few weeks later the mysterious Reichstag fire was an excuse for his anti-Communist and anti-Jewish policies. The first Nazi concentration camp, Dachau, was opened. Looking back, the gradual move towards conflict seems so clear, but at the time too many were overwhelmed by personal problems to notice what was going on.

Although this really was a depressing time, it is a reminder that those born this year can see, then put right, misery caused by too much control in too few hands. Look for dictatorial patterns in your own life and consider what actions you have taken to offset them. The bottom line of your task is about power, and the need to share it. As you may have learned already, money is not the real solution to security. Your purpose is much more subtle than that. Overcoming disappointments and set-backs takes courage and a willingness to forgive, so when Saturn and Neptune met in 1989 the time had come to do both.

1934

As years go, this one posed unusual difficulties for developing self-confidence. There is an overall hint that whatever is attempted will produce a feeling that it is too little, too late. That comes from being inadequately prepared because of either a reluctance to face facts or an unwillingness to change the old rules. The slow planets were like the sails of a windmill out of alignment and blown from too many directions at once. It was a frightening time and even nature was the enemy with dust storms and grass-hoppers ruining North American harvests.

Pluto in conflict with both Saturn and Uranus, brought political frustration or a sense of powerlessness. In many countries opponents of those in power were being eliminated, imprisoned or starved. And as unemployment increased desperate individuals banded together forming mass movements which caused authorities to use harsh methods to control them. As Saturn in Aquarius was leaving the uncomfortable aspect (inconjunct) with Neptune, left over from last year, it met the irritation of another inconjunct from Pluto. Feelings were pitted against sensible planning as Neptune undermined self-assurance and Pluto in Cancer encouraged lack of security which produced anger. The public's ability to stand up for what it believed, without looking the other way, or waiting too long to act, was being tested. That is a key note of your year.

This was the time to avert the next war but not enough people were paying attention, or else were too busy trying to survive. Dictators' aims became obvious with Stalin purging his rivals; Hitler murdering army leaders in the Night of the Long Knives and Himmler's SS commanding the concentration camps. Oswald Moseley's blackshirts demonstrated in London; martial law was proclaimed in Spain; and so on and so on. Perhaps the increase of cruelty and domination could have been "nipped in the bud" but most governments did not want to see.

The message for you to follow is that your efforts to withstand what you know to be wrong do matter however trivial they might appear at the time. The appropriate proverb would be "a stitch in time saves nine."

Where Pluto is concerned big bucks are often involved and this year, with its waning square to Uranus, saw the old methods of controlling finance challenged while economic manipulation was rife. This was the last square of a long cycle which began with their conjunction in Taurus around 1851 when slavery was a big issue and soon after a California gold strike. The consciousness raising of a waning square should have signaled the dangers of subjugation and concentration of riches. In the US the Gold Reserve Act and the formation of the Federal Reserve placed power in a few private hands not accountable to anyone. The price of gold was fixed but the dollar devalued to 60 cents. The Aquarian president, FDR, was being undermined.

A dominating energy this year was the Aquarian Saturn, an original mind haunted by tradition. Usually aware of its responsibility to the collective, it can be intimidated by crowds yet not want to be a lone voice. A way out of that tension can be to direct your considerable will-power to building on new ideas rather than always siding with authority. An opportunity to do so could have occurred in 1962 when Saturn was again inconjunct Pluto this time from Aquarius to Virgo. The warning here was to accept responsibility where you thought it was warranted and not get downhearted when you are criticized. 1992 brought another Saturn return and renewed opportunity for wise progress.

1935

The struggles continue, bringing hardship, confusion and escapism. Like other years in the '30s this was not a particularly happy time to be born but with the international tensions imprinted on your psyche, you are a good candidate to help put them right in your lifetime. As we all prepare for a new age in the Global Village, your empathy could be instrumental in finding an answer to the impatience some people have with the powerless and the destitute, as it is a problem that societies must solve to be healthy.

Like last year, Saturn is once again in difficult positions. Squaring Chiron it poses questions about authority, whether to feel suppressed by it or try to dodge its rules. In either case there needs to be some compromise as none of us can by-pass responsibility entirely. Saturn in Pisces (reality confused) as it was for most of the year, and Neptune in Virgo (loss of confidence) could be at the heart of any anxiety. But both can be turned into practical success if your creative imagination (Pisces) is used to be productive (Virgo). The nervousness of Chiron in Gemini can cause hang-up about thinking realistically if you sense that you are not being offered the whole truth and nothing but the truth. The desire to escape reality was growing and Hollywood was increasing its production of fantasy and Follies.

Temperamental undercurrents can be sources of inspiration or panicky feelings and those born this year will be challenged to take control of them. With this mixture of earth and water you can either sink into mud and succumb to depression, or mold dreams into tangible shapes like a potter.

Eclipses throw the spot-light on to leadership revealing how power is being used, and there were seven eclipses this year. Emotions were running high and fear increased as world leaders made their moves in the power games. Hitler marched into Austria, Mussolini invaded Ethiopia and Mao Tse Tung finished his "long march" in China. The League of Nations, which had been formed to preserve peace, was unable to stop any of them. In the US Roosevelt's New Deal to help the unemployed was being opposed. Nature was on the move too. In April there was Black Sunday, when dust swept through Oklahoma "like a tidal wave of earth.".

Late 1959 into 61 it was time to get serious. Transiting Saturn in Capricorn and Pluto opposing your Saturn, perhaps backed you into a corner to reconsider any illusions you had been harboring. Then at your first Saturn return in 1964, came a time to test your sense of reality when Uranus, now in Virgo near your Neptune, was providing the urge to change whatever rules you felt were holding you back. By your second Saturn return, in 1994, both Uranus and Neptune opposed your Pluto, highlighting any insecurities you had refused to face. Aspects to Pluto help to reveal the shadow side that everybody has but is loathe to inspect. To admit faults, particularly obsessions, to ourselves can be such a relief as it then saves all that energy we spend in pretending they do not exist. Painful though learning may have seemed, the slow planets provided years of apprenticeship helping you to reshape your life with precision, like a sculptor producing a masterpiece, or the director of an Oscar-winning film.

1936

This was another testing year in which a lack of reality provoked idealists into actions that failed. It was a year for sacrifices and short-lived triumphs which do not mean that motives were not good but that goals were just not achievable unless enough support had been lined up ahead of time. Your lesson here is to check, check and check again before launching into your "good works". The demand for controlled realism found in last year's pattern of planets was now reinforced by an extra need for organization and common sense. Neptune was front and center, while still opposed by Saturn, making it hard to determine truth from wishful-thinking. Also Jupiter was encouraging greater efforts but possibly adding to the confusion with its over-optimism.

The keynote here is beware of going too far too fast and to look ahead before stepping off into space. Your long-term plans should be soundly based with plenty of back-up from potential fence-sitters who believe in you but are reluctant to get involved. Success comes from persuading them first, then acting as a team.

When you were born extremism was pulling people apart, with right wing vs. left wing and illusions vs. disillusions canceling out the efforts to preserve sane societies. As evidence of the brutality sweeping Europe became clearer, the number of concerned people increased. Some joined in the Spanish civil war, which was the dress rehearsal for WWII, but still too many preferred to look the other way, hoping the growing nightmare would just go away.

Anxiety and guilt are part of Neptune's bag of tricks but this was no time to doubt that wrongs can be put right if tackled soon enough. Creativity aligned with practicality could have replaced old dreams with radical new ones if only more interest had been mobilized.

Take a tip from some of the events that may have seemed successful at the time but could not stand up to the wear and tear of reality. Edward VIII nearly became king but abdicated before his coronation "for the woman I love". And that turned out to be a disappointing match. Mussolini, conquering the Abysinians thought "Italy now has its empire" and that did not last long. The Nazis entered the Rhineland and Germany and Japan signed an anti-Communist pact. Both countries paid the price, eventually. This is hardly a list of permanent successes!

An opposition of Saturn (in Pisces) to Neptune (in Virgo) needs a lot of practical cooperation to be successful and the history of this year is a reminder of that. Some social experiments were tried but usually without adequate support. Attempts to introduce financial balance came from social welfare advocates, and people like Eleanor Roosevelt tried hard to establish self-sufficient communities.

Quite early in your life, you might have rooted out an emotional undercurrent that was leading to problems. What happened in 1954-55, when Uranus, on your Pluto was shaking up your insecurity while it was being squared by confusing Neptune? Then in 1986 Pluto opposed Uranus, a challenge to any stubbornness preventing you from moving forward. By 1987-88, with Uranus squaring Uranus, major changes in your self-evaluation could have given you more freedom to enjoy being yourself, without anxiety or illusion.

1937

This was the year of an interesting metaphor from Hollywood. Snow White, the innocent child was nearly destroyed by a wicked step-mother but the dedicated dwarfs (the workers) brought her back to life, eventually. The message here is beware of dictators, and manipulative controllers, and rely on the loyalty of the "common man/woman", willing to oppose as a team, what seems frightening.

While Neptune was still in Virgo opposite Saturn, there was still far too much anxiety, frustration and escapism around. This lesson, similar to that for the last few years, was not to close your eyes to trends you just do not want to see. The honest ambition of Jupiter in Capricorn, in opposition to Pluto can turn into a destructive push for power if it lands in the wrong hands. The cosmic hints of the two oppositions are to remind you of the dangers of innocence, or ignorance, and to beware of allowing others too much control over you. Your security depends on being cooperative, not pushy or pushed around.

Dictators were in the limelight with German bombers joining the Spanish war and Japan invading China. Stalin shot many of his generals who opposed his ruthlessness. Buchenwald camp was opened and a massive Nazi rally was held in Nuremberg. In hindsight it should have been impossible to avoid seeing the darkness descending, unless one was condoning it.

In your maturity you may still be faced with problems concerning work and workers but will have the capacity to recognize the value of looking for meaning in a job, rather than just an income.

For those of you with a grand earth trine of Jupiter, Uranus and Neptune, common sense about welfare or charity could come naturally in labor-relations. Something you could do well is help the disadvantaged without destroying their independence and individual ability to live life for themselves. The delicate balancing act of respecting human dignity while enhancing the productivity of those in need by "teaching a man to fish" is a solution you understand.

In the early '60s Neptune was challenging your sense of freedom as it opposed your Uranus. Then the first Saturn return came, in 1967, with more than its usual call for responsibility, coinciding with a Uranus and Pluto conjunction that only occurs about every 127 years. How you reacted to the sixties revolution will tell you a lot about yourself. Were you ready to go forward into a different kind of future, with Uranus, or be held back by anxiety, with Neptune? Uranus provided new ideas but Neptune often led to the psychedelic escape. A lot of genuine idealism got lost in the drug scene but it was ready for resurrection in the '90s, by your second Saturn return when Neptune was opposite your Pluto, reviving ambition to do something worthwhile.

Questions left over from the "dirty thirties" are still applicable today. When the props are taken away many people fall down. As a positive legacy of such difficult times you can achieve stability yourself and show others how to approach work differently. Your life pattern certainly put good judgment to the test early, perhaps before you were ready to take responsibility. But having another chance in the '90s, at your second Saturn return, offers a happy ending.

1938

The character of the year is a clear illustration of your basic conundrum. First assuming a crisis is over then having to face the mistakes of not dealing with it sooner. Neptune's ability to confuse decisions posed a threat and a frustrated, or frustrating, Saturn in Aries may be slow to adjust to its deception.

Like last year's children, you spent your early adulthood in the midst of the '60s craziness and had to choose between going forward or backward. At that time Pluto was crossing your Neptune, always an invitation to dig up illusions and revise dreams. With Neptune's dissolution of old forms, Saturn rebuilds them, and though the voices of many idealists got drowned out in the hysteria of the late '60s and '70s, they did not go away. To make yourself heard in the '90s you just had to shout a bit louder, if you wanted to be helpful.

Stepping back to view the big picture shows that the rise of communism and fascism was a terrible reaction to economic tribulations, obsessive beliefs and poor information. In this long Neptune-Pluto cycle, begun at the end of the last century, there was bound to be confusion (Neptune) and destruction (Pluto) before a healthy climate could be established. For the last half of this century these two energies, in sextile, have been developing a widening awareness of the need for faith and power-sharing among those willing to search for spiritual meaning.

Pluto was in Cancer between 1914 and 1939 focusing on security. By late 1938 it was preparing to enter Leo, the sign of strong wills. From then on, the clash of dictators taught us the danger of ego-domination, so that succeeding generations could learn to use their power for the good of the mass with an idealism that avoided fanaticism.

The discord of Saturn in Aries (negative action) inconjunct Neptune in Virgo (deception of self) is a good description of the year's history. Hitler invaded Austria then managed to con Neville Chamberlain, the British prime minister, who had his illusions of "peace in our time". Four days after the Munich pact was signed Hitler dropped his pretense and took over Sudentenland then Czechoslovakia. A fait accompli that showed his true colors.

Unemployment was still terribly high on both sides of the Atlantic but that was about to change when international aggression was too obvious to ignore. Preparations for war would solve the problems of the jobless. Having to manufacture arms to keep a society economically healthy is a bittersweet conclusion and an oxymoron. That is a warning that realism and good planning can save a lot of heartache.

Just before your first Saturn return, around 1968, soon after Pluto and Uranus had shaken up your Neptune, was a time to check how you were dealing with disappointments. Considering the social chaos of that era it would not be surprising if they had produced fears and frustration. Between 1995-98 your Pluto power was challenged by oppositions from Uranus then Neptune near the end of Capricorn and into Aquarius, giving you choices to be serious or escapist. Then Saturn made its second return at a time that it was wise to be well-informed instead of falling for rumors. Mirroring the tenor of the doubt and ignorance in your year of birth those two testing periods were very useful for your self-knowledge. After them, future actions could be based on serious beliefs, not fairy tales.

1939

The year of 1939 ushered in an era of strong wills and, inevitably, the conflicts that go with them. It also synchronized historically with 1914, 1968-69 and the end of the century when attitudes to warfare were about to change. With Pluto in Leo, for most of the year, and with Saturn squaring it in the last few months, the world stage was set for a knock-down-drag-'em-out power play with ego drives at full throttle. A good overture for your year was a song popular in the '70s, "Here come the Lions" which described people born with the strong egos of Pluto in Leo. But that square adds or subtracts from the intense confidence that should go with it. Conflict with authority or a denial of responsibility could lower the awareness of your power.

You are part of a generation which had to learn that being a leader is more than grabbing the place at the head of the line. Flaws of pride or greed can be dangerous if not tamed, and lions do like to have their own way! Without restraint any ego can lose touch with reality and float off on some self-indulgent folly and, beginning this year, such temptations increased.

With so many planets in fixed signs there is an innate determination among your peers to get their own way. For some of you it may seem easy and, perhaps, power has been dropped into your lap without you having to go to much trouble. Lucky you, but that is only the sugar-coating The obligations are correspondingly great — like noblesse oblige. It is a safe bet that at some time during your life you tried the negative way of pushing your own wishes against others with weaker wills. You may have won, of course, but what did you win? Looking after yourself and your own pleasures is not your ultimate goal. You, along with the rest of humanity, were due to evolve through difficult times.

Another world war was about to continue the lesson started in 1914 illustrating the futility of killing for "what's mine", whether it is for security, family, nation or culture. The first six years of your life proved that the price of fighting was too high. That is a lesson that had already taken humanity half a century to learn and would go on for another half, at least. You can teach others that confrontation is wasteful. Defense and aggression are different states of mind and there are better ways of standing up for principles than throwing grenades around to get what you want. So consider yourself a good candidate to pioneer the abolition of war and arms sales because you know, instinctively, disputes cannot be settled permanently that way.

This was an unforgettable year with its long-lasting impact. Hollywood made the Wizard of Oz and Gone with the Wind, while technology being developed for war brought accelerated changes that led Man to the Moon!

A Saturn return in 1969 brought you difficult choices, as it did for younger people who had to decide whether to fight or not to fight — in Vietnam. Your decisions then may have had some impact on 1983-84 when both Saturn and Pluto together squared your Pluto, defining important responsibilities. When your next Saturn cycle began, in 1998, Neptune was opposing your Pluto, cleansing deep-seated problems and revealing an interest in spirituality. A major lesson being played out in the Balkans, where the 1914 war began brought a cycle of power and revenge full circle. Your urge for freedom and change, Uranus, energized by the last solar eclipse of the century, in 1999, opens up leadership roles for those who have the confidence to start life's new chapter.

1940

The Great Conjunction of Jupiter and Saturn this year, produced expectations leading to delays and frustrations and, eventually, to expanding social consciousness. (This is the 20-year pattern coinciding with the legend of American presidents dying while in office). Each time this conjunction occurs it begins a new cycle of social responsibility. As the planets were in Taurus, people born this year and through May of 1941, brought with you an awareness of the resources and the environment of our planet, implying that in your lifetime any excessive materialism has to be overcome. You, personally, have an interesting choice between being ecologists par excellence or, heaven forbid, greedy for possessions. Your role is to be good stewards of the earth's natural assets.

A first test may have come around 1947 with both Pluto and Saturn squaring the point of the conjunction. Though you would have been too young to appreciate it, that time could have been significant in directing you one way or the other. To check your present values it is worth contemplating any memories you have of that period. Your principle cleaning-out-time came at the end of 1988 into 1989. Pluto was opposite that conjunction and the world was becoming increasingly aware of the dangers of yuppiedom, with too much in the hands of too few. Remember the financial take-overs and insider trading? That time could have shown most of you how well you are responding to your social responsibilities.

This year saw an amalgamating of dictators when Hitler made pacts with Mussolini and Stalin. To Britain's consternation the set-backs grew with more German invasions in Europe and the withdrawal of troops from Dunkirk, leaving the expectation of a German invasion of Britain. Then came the sinking of supply ships and, in July, the first major air raids. It was a pessimistic time and those born this year have a pattern in your birth charts of fear of deprivation coupled with determination coming from Saturn first inconjunct Neptune then forming a waning square to Pluto and finally conjoining Jupiter. Depending where you lived as a small child you may have been surrounded by uncertainty and losses as the horror of war replaced the early sense of adventure in Europe. In this "war to end all wars" it was not just the military that suffered. Families "back home" got bombed too.

Uranus in sync with Neptune, in an earth trine, suggested that your dreaming can be practical. By the mid-1990s, when these two planets met (once every 172 years), the lesson of making the best of whatever you have should be obvious. In order to help humanity, you needed to understand the confusion between caring and martyrdom and realize that there are many heart-rending situations which you can do nothing about, such as civil wars, dramatic poverty and injustice, except to keep as well-informed as possible. By tending your own garden, symbolically, and being careful not to add to other people's agony you are capable of effecting world events for the better in a practical manner. That means influencing people by example instead of interference, which is the Neptune lesson of our times and people born in 1940 could be in the vanguard of applying it.

1941

If 1941 was your year of birth expect the unexpected. Your special task could be a contest between illusion and faith and the need to make individual choices between rushing after fantasy or developing your spirituality. A solar eclipse beside Neptune, in Virgo, added focus to a spiritual opportunity to serve unselfishly at sometime during your life.

Like those a year older, you too have visions of instituting a more sensible approach to materialism into society as you were born at the time of great physical destruction. With Saturn, the planet of responsibility, still in Taurus the sign of money and possessions, and Jupiter and Uranus there part of the year, the goodies you want are likely to be tangible ones, but with Saturn you have to earn your rewards. If you have a fear of losing things, or status, you may be expending too much energy on the material side of life and not realizing that you have hidden resources in your own character.

It was a strange year to be a helpless baby and with Chiron conjunct your Pluto in Leo, some wound to your ego could have undermined your confidence. But in 2000 when they are together again, this time in Sagittarius, your optimism can be reborn.

By 1969, when Pluto joined your Neptune in Virgo, your "better angels" could have taken charge, unless anxiety over rode your natural instincts to be helpful. If that happened, watch out for allergies which are a way of telling yourself that you are not perfect. No, you are not, but neither is anyone else.

After the tensions of 1940, the second half of 1941 saw unexpected changes, with first Jupiter then Uranus moving into Gemini, adding new thinking. Those of you who arrived then might be more restless than your placid peers born a few months earlier. All 1941 people have opportunities to blend compassion with business under the earthy influence of Saturn and Neptune. How well you do this will have become obvious by 1989 when these two planets came together in the responsible sign of Capricorn.

In history, spring 1941 was the low point of the war for Britain with destructive air-raids and resource shortages from loss of shipping. Europe was under Hitler's thumb until he turned on his ally and invaded the USSR. An eclipse in September, involving Neptune (illusions) strengthened Japan's own Neptune leading it on an unrealistic path when, in December, it attacked Pearl Harbor bringing the United States into the war.

People born in this year have had to learn that you need proven facts to back up your dreams. At some time of your life a situation may have turned into a confusing maze with the goals you were pursuing always just around the next corner, or else were so numerous it was difficult to decide which were the most important. If 1985 was a year of tension, you were undergoing a sort of second puberty which showed how to be a cooperative partner, with Saturn opposing your Uranus. To understand the basic cause of tensions think back to 1971-72 and 1981. Somewhere in those two periods lie clues to your individual purpose.

By 1995-6 with Pluto opposing your Jupiter-Uranus you will surely have understood the message of combining strength with ideas. At the beginning of the next century, Saturn is back again to check on your slow planets with Uranus squaring them. Chiron-Pluto are together again and Neptune opposes them in your chart. That is a strong test to assure you are using power caringly and enjoying it.

1942

For the first five months of this year, three major planets — Saturn, Uranus and Neptune, dominated the scene. Strong wills representing the past (Saturn) had to deal with the rebellious urge for something new (Uranus), both believing they are right and often deceiving themselves, or being deceived (Neptune). The urge to stop (Saturn) and the urge to go (Uranus) met, for the first time in 45 years, at the end of Taurus, then both moved into Gemini in May, with Jupiter already there. This encouraged more objectivity, with brain power replacing muscle power, and brought in a group of souls willing to be flexible and think themselves out of difficulties rather than being self-defensive.

The year saw a beginning of fundamental changes in values, perhaps too subtle to notice at the time. Some of the same Neptune confusion that would be faced by last year's babies, lasted through September. With so much Taurus and Gemini influence, character development for those born this year would come from first confronting then pulling back to review the difference between your wants and your needs. When old traditions are shaken up by a growing yearning for freedom the upheavals can be quite violent. 1988, with another Saturn-Uranus conjunction, this time at the end of Sagittarius, could have brought a moment of truth about that for you.

The eclipses this year were interesting, five altogether which is not too unusual, but two of them fell on significant degrees with a solar eclipse at 17 Virgo gathering power for the 1965 vital Uranus-Pluto conjunction in the same place. The degree of the other solar eclipse at 18+ Leo is repeated in the dramatic patterns of August 1999 when Mars, Saturn, Uranus, and the eclipse form a fixed square. Just as 1942 was a turning point of war, 1999 is also primed for an important international choice and perhaps a personal one for you.

A lot was changing in 1942. Forces everywhere were mobilized and this was a time of massive and decisive battles — the Battle of the Atlantic, the Battle of Midway and the Battle of Stalingrad. As you were born into such an aggressive time it is wise to consider your motives if you find yourself in battles that test your determination. Force is not always the best way to win.

The years 1993-95 may have produced several reality checks of your progress that will help, if you need help, to break through any tendency to hold on to old fears. Transiting Saturn made a waning square to your Saturn-Uranus conjunction then Pluto opposed it, offering awareness of how you were dealing with the stop-go tensions in your life. The habit of defending yourself in a bull-dog fashion could be a pattern until you learn to relax and share the burden of responsibility.

Yours was a year for re-assessing whether to fight or cooperate. Although it was not apparent for months, the tide was turning away from the aggressors in favour of the allies. Increased production of weapons and secret testing of rockets in Germany was leading to the ultimate lesson of Hiroshima. From the hindsight of the 1970s and '80s, war would be viewed as too costly a means of settling disputes. It would take a Vietnam debacle to show that, but you knew it form the start, unconsciously perhaps. And therein lies the symbolism of your year. By nature you are equipped to be peaceniks.

1943

A very bright group of babies was born this year, with quick and well-organized minds and a variety of priorities. You may have been hard to teach, being precocious kids, and probably grew up with a built-in sense of rebellion ready to elevate your interest in self to a more universal plane, with Uranus in a waning sextile to Pluto, tidying up a cycle started nearly a hundred years ago. A similar request to break through the boundaries of the "little self" and develop the "Higher self was coming from Chiron conjunct the North Node in Leo. If you have responded to these demands to grow spiritually your evolutionary instinct could be particularly strong making you important initiators of new values needed for the next century.

It was a mixed bag of a year astrologically and physically. On the world stage the initiative was gradually shifting from the aggressors to the defenders. Jupiter conjunct Pluto added force to resistance, and progress in resisting the dictators was showing. Sicily was invaded; Mussolini was forced to resign and Hitler's Germany was being bombed unmercifully as the Russians started to push the Germans back. With Saturn and Uranus coming together in Gemini new technology was taking effect and many of you born now would have no trouble making sense of computers when they arrived. Some of you would act impatiently if your Mars was in Gemini too, and had to learn to slow down and have faith to avoid falling over your own feet trying to "do good". If you had trouble early in life expressing ideas or your needs there could have been some communication block, preventing others seeing how really bright you were.

One of your life tasks could be to communicate what some cannot explain for themselves. When anyone is misunderstood repeatedly, frustration can explode into anger and people born at any time this year could have a special empathy for such situations. An ideal chance to be sympathetic came in 1972-73, at your Saturn return when Neptune was opposite. Again in 1985-88 when both Saturn and Uranus opposed your Saturn, encouraged you to reach out to meet others at least half way. That would have been a good time to be philosophical and share your wisdom.

One sign that may not have had a problem explaining itself is Leo. You Leos of this year are very demanding, and probably made your needs understood one way or another right from the start with Jupiter and Pluto together in your sign. That spells POWER, in capital letters, and calls for a special kind of leadership.

The best use of the major planets, for those born this year, will be to accept the responsibility of leadership that combines knowledge (Uranus) social concern (Neptune) and strong will (Pluto). That could put you way out front unless you fell into the Leo trap of selfishness. You were not meant to have everything your way and the ego tests of Saturn in Leo squaring Uranus as it moved into Scorpio, dampened down your Jupiter. This happened in 1975 through 1976 when a harsh lesson could have curbed any unnecessary excess you had developed.

In the last two years of the century it was time to be objective and see yourself through interaction with others. Saturn opposing your Neptune was testing a sense of reality about partnerships, while Uranus opposite your Pluto and Pluto opposite your Uranus were checking your visionary ideas.

1944

This was not an easy year to be born. There was plenty of tension everywhere with the war still raging around the world and millions of bombs being dropped on many countries. A sense that it was all going on too long did strange things to hope. Sometimes the end seemed to be in sight then vanished. It was a powerful year with all four of the slow planets making mid-point combinations with each other and a roller-coaster anxiety, with Saturn in a waning square to Neptune. This has probably shaped your psyche in some way either making you feel pressured or wanting to withdraw to somewhere quiet for a time and that is a good antidote for your tension. The world is not against you, though occasionally you might have thought it was.

This year's crop of babies was born with the ability and ambition to lead, plus the brain power to be quite original, though there could be some difficulty in communicating ideas in simple enough terms for us normal-sized brains to understand you. If you felt held back as kids you may resent authority but you did need a little reining in to slow down and deepen your thinking rather than let it wash all over the place. You could have all kinds of answers to problems and want to share them but be unable to understand an "ordinary Jo's" point of view. Unless you have a lot of your personal planets in water signs (Cancer, Scorpio and Pisces) your big hang-up will be your feelings. Being a bit insensitive to other people's you may not be very good at conveying yours to them.

You have come through interesting years and reviewing them may help to make sense of a few unconscious instincts. If you kept a dream diary, 1981 would be the year worth exploring with the Great Conjunction of Jupiter and Saturn happening on your Neptune. By then it was time to release your hidden longings. Perhaps something that happened that year can be associated with a feeling of being let down by reality. If so you might consider that to be a hint that you were ready for some spiritual growth, opening a door to hidden feelings and inner strengths.

The Conjunction itself is the start of a new cycle for social improvements, this time for Libra diplomacy, justice and cooperation but its half-way point brought the Gulf War so something was not going according to the Universe's plan. For you, personally it allowed inspiration to seep into your active mind giving you an opportunity to enjoy life's finer things like music and art, in a new way. Then came 1986, a year for mind-changing with oppositions of the two contradictory planets. Saturn opposed your Uranus and Uranus opposed your Saturn. And simultaneously, Neptune squared your Neptune and Pluto squared your Pluto, two major crises offering fine-tuning for your spirituality and power. Surely that was a time of important tests that would have helped you break through any deep-seated tensions?

Life ain't perfect, but it is not all bad either. Your big-heartedness, coming from Jupiter in Leo, or even Virgo, can help dry tears by 1998-9 when you have a pocketful of trines with Uranus and Neptune in Aquarius trining your Uranus and Neptune, and Pluto in Sagittarius trine your Pluto. You cannot want more than that.

1945

When you are born into a historic year like 1945, a turning point for the world, it is obvious that you have a special significance. And it is more than usually important to understand what it is you came to do. You were the forerunners of a wave that was about to engulf us all in the following years, when the baby boomers arrived. Pluto at the midpoint of Uranus/Neptune brings a loud wake-up call to break old patterns and accept reform and new ideas however much you might want to resist them.

During your life you have probably experienced many situations which put you in conflict with the past, or with tradition. Because of this, with Saturn in Cancer square Neptune and near the mid-point of Uranus/Pluto, you might have a fear of being separated from the old and familiar and want to hang on to emotional situations for the wrong reasons. An obsession with security could be rooted in that anxiety, giving the family too strong an influence on you. If so, you may have tried to be what parents, or your culture, expected you to be even though you were not happy in that role. Sharing ideals with others who would never pass your family's test of respectability, you might have added to your social tensions and wondered which way to go, with parents or with your peers. The best solution would have been to avoid extremes be conventional sometimes and contemporary at others. Whichever way you choose, Saturn, the boomerang, will bring its rewards or its penalties.

The summer's lunar eclipse in Capricorn, square Neptune, and solar eclipse beside Saturn, were reminders to accept responsibility for establishing security, or pay a high price. Though such strong Saturn influence may have its emotional frustration it gives the inclination to be the wise banker, building your castles slowly as protection for others.

The year started with some of the toughest fighting of the war, both in Europe and the Far East, ending in Europe with VE Day, in May, and in the Far East, with VJ Day in August, after the dropping of two atomic bombs. The mixture of shock and relief, over Hiroshima left behind difficult questions of principle. From then on, knowing about the bomb and about death camps, humanity had to face the fact that it had the power to destroy itself and the planet, plus the ruthlessness to do it.

Conflicting principles are what you have had to face and it is futile to run away from the choices. That is what your year was all about. Through the '90s Saturn opposed your Neptune, and Uranus your Pluto, preparing for Pluto's opposition to your own Uranus in 2000 or 2001, when new wisdom would be available to add to, or challenge, your values.

All this symbolized the pull between past and future that you have experienced in your life, perhaps many times. It also implies that you have the means to initiate new attitudes to world security. History did not give you a particularly safe foundation, and that is hard on characters who want to be dependent. But by denying you security, in its old meaning of being able to rely on things staying the same forever, fate was doing you a good turn. Things had to change to make room for healthy growth and 1945 was a turning point, offering new opportunities.

The three spring full moons of any year are important times for spiritual growth but this year was exceptional. In the esoteric teachings of Alice Bailey and the Theosophists, the planetary patterns were focusing on the need to realign consciousness within our solar system and rebalance our own planet with peace and harmony. Seeds of a cosmic plan were being planted to increase the Light (Uranus), Love (Neptune) and Power (Pluto) on earth. The spring of 2000, with its concentration of planets in earth signs shows what progress has been made.

1946

Post-war babies were the first of the Boomer generation and they carried within them a capacity for reforming society's conception of power. From this year onward, the real leaders of the next century were about to be born. The two planets closely associated with the Shadow side of our psyche, Saturn and Pluto, were preparing to meet (next year) for the first time in 32 years, for a crucial test of leadership.

Leo, where the conjunction would take place, is the most self-involved sign, and Pluto is the most destructive of urges, so the lives of people born in the next three years were going to produce a rather dangerous choice of how the power given to them would be played out through power-tripping or power-sharing — for self or for the good of the whole. In this closing year unconscious stirrings about the responsibilities of power were growing. This makes your inner voices important, so listen to them. A time of major decisions was approaching with a scramble for advantage in the yet-to-be-born Israel, and an India being torn apart. The divisions in Europe were described as an Iron Curtain and the trials at Nuremberg were illustrating difficult moral choices. Inevitably, difficult choices would have to be made when you became the authorities in charge. It would not be surprising if you experienced crises happening to you in 1978 to 1980, when Uranus was squaring your Pluto and Neptune opposing your Uranus, so the basic urge of freedom to be yourself was undergoing some emotional trauma. Consider the motivations for the choices made around that time.

This was the start of the "Me First" generation and, for many of you, your early years were spent throwing out the old customs and shocking your elders in attempts to break up rigid systems. Earlier generations had their own lessons to learn. Your year was the start of what Marshall McLuhan, Canada's famous futurist, called the "television generation" which would lead us towards the global-village approach to international affairs. Because you had access to so much information many of you could be politically hyper, as was the youngest American president, Bill Clinton and his entourage. That does not mean you were always wise about using means for certain ends, the big lesson for your generation.

While still young you had the difficult choice of whether to fight or not fight. To your credit many recognized the futility and manipulation of war (in Vietnam) as something to abhor. So the first tear of loyalty to a flag was made by the first post-Hiroshima generation. When Pluto's effect grew stronger as it moved into its sign of Scorpio in 1984, Uranus opposite Uranus brought your mid-life crisis that would determine which individuals would move forward to greater power and which ones had developed the blinders Leo wears if it is entirely absorbed in self. The former ones would be capable of leading the world to a new form of community, while the latter could wallow in self-indulgence. Another choice would be to work for something you believed in, but behind the scenes.

The whole of the baby boom generation will nudge out old power structures if only because of its size. So a big turn-around of public approach to values and behavior should results from the effects of your maturity, and be visible by the end of this century. For those born with Saturn in Leo, a waxing square from Jupiter in Scorpio every 12 years brings a crucial test of will. You are the initiators of many of the lessons the world has to learn to avoid destruction.

1947

Last year started a different trend of post-war thinking, but this year was climactic. The planets of control, Saturn and Pluto, conjoined at 13 degrees of Leo when the Sun, Mercury and Venus were also there, making this a very personal exercise in handling the superego. The last time these planets met was in Cancer in 1914, so that cycle of control was about security, a lesson which took two world wars to learn. This lesson is about pride and ego-power. An interesting symbol of this was the breaking of the sound barrier in October. As the world moved into the Supersonic realm it seemed that some obstruction to an unknown world had been breached. All year, mysterious flying objects, (later called UFOs) were sighted and a space-ship wreck and bodies were alleged to have been found in New Mexico.

Synchronizing with this drama was a rising fear of communism. This was the time that people were considering whether it was "better to be dead than Red". How paranoid this sounds 50 years later! Patterns were changing everywhere with the Marshall Plan introducing aid to a shattered Europe; India and Pakistan splitting apart; and Einstein suggesting that it was time for a world government now that the atomic age had ended nationalism. Unfortunately, it had not. Post-war wounds were painful and Chiron in Scorpio, with its own strong feelings, was squaring Pluto, risking more poison or pollution in the areas of power.

People born this year have the seeds of drama within them with so much Leo and Scorpio influence, and a tremendous drive to succeed. But in what? For many of you it could be a kind of anti-success, as you were determined to make life as difficult as possible and may have used lots of energy *not* getting to the top. Being the kids who rebelled against the comforts of home, the sweet phoniness of the fifties with the bobby-soxers and hula hoops, many of you protested by leaving home to live in communes or hitch-hike round the world, in considerable discomfort.

Were you testing the power of tradition and trying to break through a persistent barrier that separated your conscious ego from your unconscious self which you really did not understand? If a lot of your life has been a struggle, you may have been fighting against yourself with stubbornness replacing determination. There may be many occasions you have sabotage yourself by holding on too long. If you have felt that society is trying to control you against your will you may overreact by using a sledge-hammer to kill a fly.

Saturn made a waxing square to the degree of its Leo conjunction in 1984 testing your super determination, followed by Pluto doing the same thing in 1988 and 1989. By 1992 when Saturn opposed the Saturn-Pluto conjunction of your birth year, Chiron had joined the conjunction point and probably brought a report card with it exposing its vulnerability. Any extreme use of force could be covering some inadequacy and self-doubt and that is worth checking around the age of 50, the time to heal wounds by unearthing deep feelings you have had from birth. By then Chiron had returned to its natal position in Scorpio, and was squared by Uranus in Aquarius which was opposing your Pluto, a challenge to free yourself by plumbing your own emotional depths.

1948

Some of the effect of the last two years will have rubbed off on you but since several planets changed signs you could have more flexibility. A lot of you have probably been searching for perfection most of your life, not willing to accept second best. That is a difficult prescription for marriages and many of you may have held back from commitment. Relating emotionally does not come easily if your Chiron in Scorpio on your South Node holds on to old hurts out of habit instead of cleaning them out and letting bygones be bygones. If you are not undervaluing yourself, then you may be doing that to someone who wants to help.

Independence and a built-in supply of ego energy, or pride, may have kept you on a path even when the going got rough and those around you tried to persuade you that your ideas were not very practical. Perhaps they were not, always, as your Sagittarian Jupiter can be busy seeing over the next hill without bothering to notice where you put your feet.

If you believe in angels your guardian angel probably hauls you out of trouble at the last moment. There is a high level of idealism/mysticism running through the year and where that exists, it is almost inevitable that some experiences have brought you disappointments. So you really need that angel to cheer you up occasionally

Semi-squares among the slow planets, Saturn to Neptune and Uranus to Pluto, describe irritations which need attention. Some of you will have found your uniqueness through mental pursuits while others were experimenting with community living and dealing with emotional upheavals.

Yours was a year when leadership and philosophy could be nicely blended as long as the past has not held you back. You can dream even if no one wants to believe your dreams but as you mature and take over the power from older generations some of those dreams are possible. Just be willing to admit that a few are way out, specially that expectation of a perfect relationship.

Historically, your year was a difficult one. Although World War II was over, peace was not bringing the expected rewards, and pessimism and fanaticism were growing out of frustrated power plays. Much of the world was rebuilding shattered cities but divisiveness was still common. While Israel struggled to become a country, in partitioned India, Gandhi, the man of peace, was assassinated and in Germany Berlin was blockaded to separate east from west.

For many of you, 1973-74 could have brought self-doubts with Saturn in a waning square to Pluto. This was the end of Vietnam and it was time for some serious reflection. There have been several years in the 1980s when your faith was sorely tested. It may sound harsh but are you sure you do not bother about other people's problems just to escape from your own? Running away from ugliness may have been a temptation for you in your mid-thirties and if the journey included an expansion of philosophy and self-awareness it could have been a worthwhile one. But reality, and old pain, had to be faced between the ages of 45 and 50 in a deluge of Scorpio. First Pluto squared itself, and your Saturn, then joined your Chiron as Chiron itself was returning. You may be a healer but when you go visiting the needy are you sure that someone is minding *your* store.

1949

Some years the astrological message seems to fall into definite categories and some years it does not, and 1949 is one of these. People born during this year have a mixed bag of tricks in their planetary patterns, with semi-squares, sextiles and the creative seventh harmonic. Something you do share is the timing of the shake-ups which you may have noticed on and off since 1976. That was the year Pluto started to uncover any fantasy your Neptune had been harboring while Saturn, conjoining your Pluto, was ready to demolish, then rebuild, your personal ego. If you were born, with both Jupiter and Saturn in earth signs you are probably extremely conscientious about your goals, working hard and worrying often. That does not sound like much fun. At the same time you have big aspirations. Before the end of this year, Saturn at the mid-point of Neptune and Pluto warned that any dreams of power were due for analysis and criticism.

You could have shown a desire to rebel quite early in life, making it difficult for teachers, or parents, to keep up with you, so you got criticized. Maybe you thought you knew it all already, which never goes down too well with adults. Anyway, you probably worried too much and if you had any nervous troubles or allergies, anxiety may have aggravated them. By now you should have identified that problem and come up with a solution.

This same mixture of worry and drive applies to those of you born from July to the end of the year with one subtle difference. Your rebellion could have been turned against family, home or country as a way of showing that you could be independent without any help. When Uranus moved into Cancer, as it had done for a couple of months last year, the rebellion was more likely to be emotional, while other 1949ers were rebelling mentally. It would be a pity to let anxiety effect your ideas about a changing society, even though George Orwell published his book 1984 this year.

This was a year for dichotomy of past and future with Chiron in Sagittarius in difficult aspects to both Saturn and Uranus, the planets which flank it in the heavens. Optimism can be shot down easily from the wound of being "fooled before". The real meaning of Chiron's potential new wisdom is that visions, attitudes, conclusions, need revising so that the future can be seen as the outcome of the present, *not* the past. It was not the start of a new cycle on the roundabout, but one to push the spiral of hope and understanding to a new level. This is something that is repeated in the final year of this century.

A dramatic example of this was the apparent rise in communist power. While President Harry Truman was criticizing American anti-Communist hysteria, China declared itself a People's (communist) Republic, East Germany elected a communist government and Indonesia became independent under a communist, President Sukarno. Spies were being uncovered in US government and news came that Russia had "the bomb". Eventually these rigid regimes would be seen for what they were but it took years before the new tide came in. Being born this year, gives you a hint to be patient and avoid gloomy assumptions. Life is never just black or white.

In the last years of the century you were due for a test in relating with Uranus opposing your Pluto and Saturn opposing Neptune, not to mention Chiron back in Sagittarius.

1950

This was a difficult year to be born, because there were such extremes of emotion and force in the patterns of the planets and that will inevitably be imprinted on your psyche in some form. Saturn in Virgo was at the mid-point of Neptune/Pluto at the most potent degree of the signs. Whether this grouping caused you problems would depend very much on your personal chart and how aware you have been of the contradictory sides of your nature. For example, a birth in the first few months had intimations that your teenage years would contain extra emotional doubt and confusion at a time that is rife with emotion anyway, when Pluto moved on to your Saturn. If this brought frustration the problem could have developed into anger by 1972 when Uranus joined your Neptune, and clarity by 1979 when Pluto did the same thing. By that time those negatives could have been turned into the positives of sensitivity and well-directed action. If so, the rewards could have been great. If born from April onwards, when Jupiter entered Pisces, the yearning for peace grew stronger with less inclination to fight and more desire to withdraw.

Many of you may have felt over-criticized during your life, with Saturn in Virgo, and have developed a defensive mechanism. If so, any nervousness or anxiety could have caused allergies or phobias that needed to be rooted out in your teenage years when Pluto reached your Saturn. It might help to realize that your fear of criticism is probably the result of an overdose of self-criticism making any extra that is added from outside a bit too much to handle. Also, you were born into a very nervous time, historically.

Just as the world was starting to recover from WWII the Korean War broke out in June and we were back to building air-raid shelters again, this time for protection from the appalling threat of atomic war. Two interesting symbols of deception and destruction (Neptune/Pluto) were the development of the hydrogen bomb and the CIA increasing its psychic aggression. Then a polio epidemic started with its nervous rigidity and muscle waste. Is it any wonder you 1950 babies have had to contend with emotion and unconscious fears in your lives?

Suspicion and disappointment were part of your upbringing. But that is all past now as the last few years of the 1970s should have pushed you out of the anxiety rut with some kill-or-cure aspects. Neptune was squaring your Saturn, perhaps offering new faith and Saturn was meeting your Pluto, to rebuild your confidence. It was also a time when alternative healing was coming into vogue with Uranus in Scorpio, squaring your Pluto, but at the midpoint of transiting Neptune and Pluto. Those heavy squares just before your Saturn return brought a reminder to help yourself. If not, 1995 gave you an extra view, with Saturn opposite Saturn, even if you had to see it through what was happening to someone else.

The planets main design for your year (that Saturn mid-point) seems to have been a test for obsessions and illusions and a need to boost genuine faith in self rather than blaming others. This was also the start of an opportunity for people born from 1914 and through the 1920s to break out of old insecurities and adopt more futuristic views while Uranus was shaking their Pluto in Cancer so watch for attitude changes among parents and grandparents.

1951

Difficulties in relating are on your agenda, as they were for 1950. A Pisces North Node formed a yod with Neptune and Pluto, demanding careful handling of the price of sacrifice — how much to give up for someone and how much to keep for yourself.

If this year needs a headline it would probably be a "Test for Partnerships". Like people born last year you will encounter disappointments and confusion about responsibility for others. But for you they could be more emotional, probably resulting in doubt about who to trust. Your attitude to others and how willing you are to forgive mistakes will affect your peace of mind. If you consider that "no man is an island" you may have to admit that sometimes you do want to be alone. Seeking closeness and freedom at the same time is quite a problem and one you need to solve.

You were born into a period of anxiety and disappointment as peace was snatched from our grasp. With the Korean war well underway and talk of atomic bombs, a new panic was taking over. Deep shelters were being built and stocked with enough goods to last for years. Children were diving under desks in air-raid practices and first-aid courses were in full swing. Something good that came out of this time was the long-running TV series, M.A.S.H.

Like other people born from 1943 to 1957, with Neptune in Libra, you have probably searched for some kind of perfection, or escape, through a partnership, and that inevitably brings disappointment. Expectations of Jupiter in Aries and Neptune in Libra are apt to be distorted anyway. When you have dried your tears, the Neptune influence can show you that love is never wasted even though it does not turn out as expected. That requires a forgiving nature. Such tests are important for you, so do not be despondent if you seem to have more than your fair share of them. Overlooking irritating human weakness could make you stronger and better able to relate to others with a mature sense of caring. *All* human beings can be irritating at times, even you. Offering lots of patience and tender loving care could be the answer to your peace of mind. Smooth the brows and forgive, even if you do not plan to continue on the same old tread mill. Remember, anyone can make a mistake but it becomes tragedy if you keep repeating it. When disappointment is too deep, you do have to leave rather than be a victim. Leaving with a kind thought is easier on your psyche than harboring a grudge.

Turning points for you came at the beginning of the 1980s. Your Saturn return was the time of the Great Conjunction of Jupiter and Saturn, more than a gentle hint that your expectations needed to change. In 1991-92 with your Pluto squared by Pluto then opposed by Saturn, you may have suffered from a bruised ego and a realization that it was time to let go of something, or someone. Confusion about responsibilities for others was a keynote of your year.

Having an interesting Pluto, near the mid-point of Saturn/Uranus, has given you the strength to cope with set-backs, and opportunities to confront your own ego. In case you have more transforming to do, a major solar eclipse of the century, in August 1999, is right on that Pluto. That is power piled on power and even if there are no personal events involved, your influence will be useful, so be prepared to deal with the outcome calmly.

1952

This was an especially significant year for human beings to learn how to be realistic and idealistic, about themselves and others. With Saturn (limits) and Neptune (dreams) together, both interacting with Uranus (freedom) this was a time to wonder what to believe or not. You were bound to join in the search for the perfect partner that last year's kids started and next year's will continue. If results do not live up to expectations it is not fair to blame someone else for your misconceptions. Just check your illusions, forgive, yourself and others, and push on.

When the abstract feelings of Neptune bump up against Saturn's need for structure, the result can be both anxiety and frustration. Add to that the restlessness of Uranus and you have a picture of rebellious chaos. The positive side of this threesome is an opportunity for new visions and changes in political values. Take your pick. Around your early years, historical variations on this theme lasted for years with a mixture of restlessness and confusion. The British king died, and, in Africa, an early colonial rebellion started when the Mau Mau tribe wreaked havoc among English settlers. Britain introduced the first "nuke" bringing protesters out in thousands and in the United States, General Eisenhower won a landslide victory for president promising to end the Korean war. Interest in UFO's increased and George Jorgenson became Christine with the first well-publicized sex change operation.

Many of you born this year with Jupiter in Taurus, may have had that "hemmed in" feeling if you put a lot of effort into material belongings You have probably gone through periods of enjoying the good things of life and trying to hoard them, only to find that you lost out somewhere. If the rug was pulled just when you thought you had it made, you were being reminded that good things are supposed to be shared. A hard lesson and one you may have resisted. But there is always time to make amends. Your desire to do things your own way is one thing, but you could make yourself an outcast if you are too independent. Taking part in what is happening around you and being useful to society with your original ideas and ability to make something out of nothing is your challenge. From 1989, way into the '90s, your Uranus had many aspects from the outer planets with Jupiter conjoining it and Saturn, Uranus and Neptune opposing it. That sounds like a personal revolution with opportunities to achieve many of your goals as long as you sought cooperation from others.

Your strong urge for freedom could have made you break away from your family while you were still quite young. It was the flower child within you and Uranus in Cancer wanting to share closeness with friends rather than relatives. In your lifetime you will probably experience a universal shift in that direction with more and more children blaming their parents for their own problems and turning to sympathetic peers for comfort. But you need to understand that parents were responding to difficult times too. You and those born in the years around you arrived at the time of social turmoil with ideals that were just a little ahead of society.

1953

Like births in other early 1950 years you have had plenty of confusion, and perhaps disillusion, to contend with as you grew to maturity. When it came to setting your own limits things were no longer clear-cut and many of you became Flower Children and Hippies, turning society on its head with your rebellious way of life. Saturn involved with Uranus and Neptune in a difficult dance during these years points to the source of your problems as one of parenting, what you received and how you have handled that task for your children if you had any. Many of you did not, and that in turn produced a few agonies for the females in this category, like — to have or not to have? Before you pile all the blame on Mum and Dad, consider this lesson of Saturn conjunct Neptune, as one of building a new vision of family, through friends and relationships, discovering that those closest to you may not be blood-related but true kindred spirits.

You chose a time to be born when authority was about to undergo a change of attitude with Saturn at its waxing square to Uranus as it was late last year, then joining Neptune in Libra. In your childhood parents were trying to make sense of their own lives and may not have set appropriate limits for you. Many were post-war veterans catching up on lost youth, expecting instant happiness and, of course, not finding it. That kind of disappointment tends to bring some attempt to escape from reality and for many, about the time you were born, parenting was a limiting chore. For the creative people among you a hidden advantage of any parental neglect may have encouraged you to withdraw into a world of your own imagination and develop your artistic talents.

With Jupiter square Pluto, then Saturn conjunct Neptune, this was a year when secrecy and subversion was rife and the effects would take years to show up. The Rosenbergs were executed as spies and the CIA was busy experimenting with LSD and encouraging riots in Iran. Saturn's effects were not all negative and two positive achievements were the coronation of Queen Elizabeth and the climbing of Everest by Edmund Hillary. Then the Korean truce was signed after President Eisenhower threatened to use an atomic bomb and Neptune added its symbolism with his vision of Atoms for Peace.

You were born into a world that was boiling with an explosive mixture of fear, dreams and upheavals. In the early '80s at the time of your Saturn return, many of your anxieties were exposed when Pluto was joining natal Neptune and squaring Uranus. Then in the mid-90s Neptune and Uranus together squared that Neptune. Arriving in such a Neptunian era gives you a special opportunity to produce new and mystical visions and to be part of the millennial readjustments for politics, religions and relationships. But its association with Uranus predicts change, and with Saturn casts confusion about authority which you might experience in the trend of the late '90s when younger people start competing for your position before you are ready to retire.

Another driving force for you could have been Chiron in Capricorn, resembling Sisyphus pushing the stone uphill to success and having to expend more energy than you think is necessary. At the same time it was opposite Uranus, bringing tension between tradition and doing things your way, perhaps adding more stress, first with parents and later with authority. As it is also in a waxing square to your Saturn-Neptune, important dreams can be made real with a combination of discipline and idealism. Recognition of your efforts may seem slow but a break-through could have come in 1993-94 if Uranus conjunct your Chiron released any locked-in energy so that old wounds could heal, then joined Neptune for the start of a new spiritual era.

1954

That message about mystical visions for last year's children applies to many of you too with a bit more emphasis on taking initiative rather than just dreaming. This year saw the rise of collective conflict between the strong emotional needs of Neptune and the instinct of Uranus to develop that promised Brotherhood of Man/Woman, a friction that continues in births for the next three years, while they are in a waning square. According to esoteric astrology they are in each other's signs offering the souls born in the next few years the ability to blend knowledge and devotion needed to bridge the gap between the Age of Pisces and the Age of Aquarius.

This schism became obvious in the '90s when you were ready to fight your Shadow with Pluto on your Saturn and Saturn opposing your Pluto. Many of you chose a spiritual path and immersed yourselves in alternative healing while others became Yuppies, pushing the stock market to new heights. Strangely, you must have had that impetus in your blood, as there was a record-breaking rise in stock prices the year you were born with the highest yields since the exuberant '30s. Take warning that what goes up often comes down with a thud. Those of you born later in the year, with Jupiter conjunct Uranus then squaring Neptune, would find success for your dreams if they included the world, not just you. Your sense of security can come from belonging to the human community rather than any one country, race, or family. The growing extremes of society will get attention eventually and the more spiritually developed among you will be leading the way in narrowing the gaps.

There was an interesting mix of highs and lows in this dramatic year. Roger Bannister broke the four-minute mile, and the Pope crowned the Virgin Mary as Queen of Heaven. The US tested the H-bomb, launched a nuclear submarine and built its largest aircraft carrier, then cut its military numbers. The Supreme Court declared segregated schools illegal but civil unrest continued to reach boiling point. The scare of communism was growing with the McCarthy hearings, and the defeat of the French in Vietnam left a void to be filled later by an American agony that has never fully healed.

About 1985-6 Pluto was forcing your hidden Saturn up to the surface so that you could assess your personal use (or non-use if you have been afraid of it), of authority. During the '90s opportunities to break through any negative effects of your childhood lasted for several years. First you had Pluto square Pluto, a time to dig deeply into old wounds and test your unconscious ethics. The conjunction of Uranus and Neptune, of 1993, opposed your Uranus, so you could forgive or seek forgiveness for past outbursts at that time. Then these planets moved on to square your Neptune, giving you plenty of chances to sort out any illusions about where to look for security and how to use your powers for universal good. All this was followed by Uranus square your Saturn, in 1996-97, which could have been healing if you were prepared to do some rebuilding.

In many ways you are the front-runners for the kind of communities expected in the Age of Aquarius, with grass-roots groups helping rather than dominating each other. Being part of a new wave, you cannot be impatient. Hang in there. The tide will come in for you when you are ready.

1955

Many important aspects occurred this year, starting with the conflict of Uranus and Neptune, then on to crises for Jupiter, Saturn and Pluto. With such an array of strong wills, ideals and illusions this was a turbulent time, guaranteed to confuse the political and social scenes. Being the first wave of "rebels without a cause" you are a generation of individualists. Most of you wanted to make changes in society but were not sure what structures were needed to replace the old ones.

You arrived in time for the last chapter of a 172-cycle which ended in 1993. The waning squares of Uranus-Neptune, then Jupiter-Saturn were really preparing the ground for the more focused civil upheavals of the following years beginning with the Great Conjunction in 1961 in Capricorn. During your life, if you have made plans and felt disappointed, even angry, when they did not work out as expected, you were just being too impatient. All that Saturn-Capricorn influence takes time to work. Probably people younger than you eventually picked up your baton and ran with it and you had to be content to have plowed the seed bed for them to achieve new freedoms. Some of those seeds would grow into male liberation after Uranus entered Leo, just as Uranus in Cancer (from 1948) did for women's lib. Those of you born in the second half of the year when Jupiter joined Pluto, probably have more confidence than the rest. Being over-confident or too stubborn about exercising power might have caused a case of "pride before a fall". Putting too much trust in a friend or partner, with Uranus squaring Neptune, could have brought a loss that prompted you to take off the rose-colored glasses and learn to love life as it is, not what you imagined it could be.

The early '80s were years to correct such mistakes, when Saturn brought some realism to your emotions as it joined transiting Pluto over your Neptune. Always getting your own way does not bring satisfaction but giving too much of yourself away is not a good idea either.

Disneyland opened, and the strong influences of Leo and Pluto this year spawned a rise in sexuality that led to more overt entertainment, starting with Elvis. Modesty was on the way out and Neptune moving into Scorpio was a warning that obsessions, or addictions, could be destructive.

Your year has the distinction of being called the Dawn of the Space Age, with plans being made for earth-orbiting satellites. The cosmic pattern of Chiron in Aquarius opposing Uranus set up tensions between up there and down here while the Uranus-Neptune waning square was prompting a new consciousness of priorities. Symbolically, space exploration was an urge to open up spiritual horizons and link the Self with the Higher Self, rather than living on the Moon.

At your Saturn return in 1984-5, Pluto squared that opposition pushing for the right use of inner and outer space. Then in January 1986, when Uranus was semi-square Pluto, the Challenger space shuttle exploded suggesting that tension was increasing not decreasing. When Uranus opposed your Uranus in 1996-7 there were many air crashes including the TWA800 from New York. It would seem you have a purpose to bring new balance between technology and spirituality to our planet, through your Higher Self.

1956

There are many similarities to last year's summary and everyone born this year could be at the forefront of exciting changes that will bring the elusive Age of Aquarius a little nearer. A new challenge to individuality was just beginning and the baby boom numbers started to decline. All the slow moving planets were about to change signs suggesting that you were starting life off with a clear set of instructions from the galaxy. Then you had the Chiron-Uranus opposition requiring a balance of freedom for self and others.

You arrived for the final adjustment in the idealistic cycle of Uranus-Neptune and the first crisis of the Saturn-Pluto cycle which started in 1947 with the first wave of baby boomers. Uranus squaring Neptune can leave you insecure and unclear about what kind of freedom you want but the waxing square, from Saturn to your Pluto, gives you great determination. You are carrying forward a lesson about power and a need to resolve friction between responsibility and control. Be careful not to be too dictatorial, or impose your ideas on others even though they may be good ones. A little diplomacy will help.

The squares are not easy to break through, as for most of you they are in fixed signs, but 1985, with Pluto on your Neptune, digging out emotions, and Saturn again squaring your Pluto, was a good time to examine your need to control and your fear of being controlled. If you did not settle the matter then, Pluto landing on your Saturn in the mid-90s while Neptune squared Neptune and Uranus opposed Uranus, probably forced you to let illusions go.

This was a year of strong desires but also doubts, and you may be quite different inside to that tough character you are portraying outwardly. Macho was a trend creeping into fashion with black leather, brass studs, souped-up cars and males trying to be tough guys, like Marlon Brando. In a desperate exaggeration of old stereotypes, perhaps it was masculinity's fight to the death! A break-down, or break-through, of the accepted gender differences was due to start but it would be decades before people would be comfortable with real equality. You and your peers were going to experience a surge of gender liberation, in your lifetime.

Neptune's desire to escape reality was growing stronger as it prepared to move into Scorpio. By finding a peaceful center within you can tap into the creative and spiritual opportunity of its sextile aspect to Pluto and strengthen the healing power of these two slow planets. It was a time for renewed faith on this 2,500th anniversary of the birth of Buddha. Many people born in the next few years would show a natural interest in alternative medicine, and you could be pioneers.

It was a year that realigned power, with Britain, France and Israel losing ground to the US. Western domination of the Middle East oil-fields was tested with a debacle over the Suez Canal. The Hungarian uprising and unrest over civil rights in the US, showed new bids for independence among suppressed people. In most cases the results of these efforts seemed disappointing at the time. It was a period for tidying up with the Saturn-Pluto cycle ending and a new one not starting until 1982, but it was a first step towards progress. The crises in the oil fields would cause more headaches around 1972 at the semi-square of Uranus and Neptune but their cycle did not begin until 1993. Those dates probably relate closely to your life-changes too.

1957

This was a year of confrontation and change with all the slow planets settling into new signs. It was pivotal in many circumstances, blasting through old barriers and moving ahead even though results took a long time to manifest. The space race was on with the launching of the Soviet satellite, Sputnik. That was an introduction to new possibilities for global communications, though that is not how the world first saw this remarkable feat. A few months earlier a U-2 spy plane was shot down over the Soviet Union, calling into question the depth of sincerity of the American bid for peaceful cooperation.

And here lies a good clue for you. Original ideas need to be greeted with "how interesting, how can we help to improve it" instead of " how awful, I am being left behind". In other words, you were a generation born to learn the value of sharing rather than competing. To make that possible there has to be mutual trust which is what you came to establish. The traditional macho attitude between countries and opponents was ready to be overtaken by negotiation and arbitration, but it would struggle for a long time before it gave up. In confrontation, discussion and diplomacy would have to take over from body-blows to avoid mass killing. Jupiter was at the midpoint of Neptune/Pluto at the end of Virgo, a significant opportunity for future peace for those who worked hard at it.

Beginning in 1981, the social scene was set for change with the Great Conjunction of Jupiter and Saturn happening in Libra, close to your Jupiter. It would take years before a critical mass would be strong enough to force cooperation on those reluctant to give up the old ways but you can hold on to your optimism with your energetic waxing trine between Saturn and Uranus in fire signs.

For you 1984 and into '85 was a period where the need for change would be hard to ignore, with transiting Uranus encouraging your Saturn, and Pluto conjunct your Neptune, squaring your Uranus, testing your ideals.

With your Pluto in Virgo, new values, new methods, and new attitudes would be placed on employment in your lifetime. Pluto's energy can transform work from boring repetition to a healthy productivity. But first would come the unexpected, and usually painful, job losses in the '80s and '90s, all part of a new lesson that has been seen as the end of the industrial era and the baby boom. Masses of workers (Pluto in Virgo) were going to have to share the pain, then their jobs, as a way to heal employment problems.

Last year's Uranus-Neptune square was now in fixed signs, suggesting that the battle between ideas and dreams grew stronger so that the rebels born now were more inclined to have a cause and to hold their ground. This was an important turning point for civil rights. A non-segregation bill was passed in the US Congress and when students were denied access to schools at Little Rock, Arkansas, the civil rights movement exploded. Future progress was slow but continuous, and that describes your contribution.

1958

After the changes of the last couple of years, this was a time for establishing new structures in spite of the undercurrent of strong emotions. Being born this year with Jupiter, Neptune and the North Node in Scorpio adds intensity to your emotions so you can be easily hurt, or feel rejected when others do not reciprocate on the same level. Problem number one for you could be that you are not specially good at showing your feelings and end up wondering why people do not understand you. When your ego gets wounded it is doubly hard for the real you to come across clearly, and if you try to hit back the person you hurt could be yourself.

You are rather special, being the first generation able to experience the influence of the slow planets early in your life. The personal radicalism of Uranus in Leo was growing stronger and reached crisis point in the mid to late '60s, when Uranus met Pluto and squared your Saturn. Young though you were, idealistic goals were being set at that time. From 1976 to 78, with Saturn on your Uranus then your Pluto, and Uranus on your Neptune, there were plenty of opportunities to review your ideas. From 1985 they were being challenged from Uranus conjunct your Saturn, leading to your Saturn return. If you did not get the message to widen your outlook then you would have been reminded loud and clear in 1996 and '97 with two important waxing squares, Uranus square your Neptune and Pluto square itself, giving a push to correct any destructive tendencies. Just beware of being too extreme. In the '90s all your outer planets had hard aspects, which was an invitation to find creative resolutions for some universal problems.

All of you have a certain amount of strong will and may fall into the trap of thinking that you, and only you, know what is best. That narrows your view to tunnel vision if you are not careful. Your responses will be more productive if you use a bit of diplomacy and not deal with matters in black or white. Or overdo the effort. There can be too much of a good thing, remember this was the year Ford produced the Edsel!

Creative resolutions are your province, with Jupiter sextile Pluto and Saturn sextile Chiron, two opportunities to pull rabbits out of a hat, but it does pay to think of possible results before pushing ahead too quickly. In your year the council of Vatican 11 loosened the rigid bonds of catholic worship, replacing Latin as the sole language. China was taking its Great Leap Forward, moving from its agricultural base to an industrial one. The results were painfully extreme. Millions of peasants flocked to cities and by 1966, the government tried to reverse the flow exhorting the Red Guards to action, resulting in 10 years of brutality.

From mid-year, Mars hovering in Taurus and Gemini produced a new phase in military protection with the establishment of concentrated technology. North American Aerospace Defense Command (NORAD) and North American Space Agency (NASA) were established and the first satellite was launched.

The three slowest planets will again be stirring up your transpersonal patterns by 2003, with Neptune opposing your Uranus and Uranus opposing your Pluto, testing your will power, spirituality and discrimination.

1959

In many ways, this was a year of opportunities but not in the obvious sparkly, gift-wrapped variety. They were subtle. So subtle that they could slip past unnoticed or else be relegated to the it-could-have-been-worse department. But whether you know it or not you have been presented with experiences that could give you the strength of steel, after it has been tempered. This was a waxing trine from Saturn to Pluto offering a large dose of common sense. That would put you way ahead of the weaker specimens of humanity — most of us — if you pass all the tests.

Mixed in with your determination is an obsession with criticism, or self-criticism. So you could drive yourself too hard for the sake of doing a good job, long past the point when others have given up and gone off to play. Too much concentration can make people stick to a task rigidly when they should be relaxing, and if you forget to relax stiff joints or up-tight opinions can become a problem.

Discipline may have been coming from outside sources, like parents and teachers, or from your inner urge to do things right. With Saturn in the unyielding sign of Capricorn, in unison with Pluto, both in earth signs, you are nothing if not practical. In between is the dissolving effect of Neptune, adding a sensitive or psychic element to your nature.

Doubts, emotions, illusions, could confuse your ambitions and have you questioning the goals you thought were worthwhile. Most of you had rules imposed on you that did not encourage the softer, mystical energies lurking underneath. The resolution of this contradiction will depend on how sensitive you allow yourself to be to the bass motif flowing through your own concerto. Listen to your inner self and you will do just fine.

You arrived at the same time as the Cuban revolution and the Chinese invasion of Tibet. Two unresolved power plays, which went sour but are still on the world's agenda.

The historical and personal crises can be solved once the subtleties are accepted and it is realized that all is not as it appears on the surface.

Most of you born this year have some distinct leadership qualities, once you have got yourself together. Nobody can lead well until they feel centered and comfortable with themselves and though at times you might feel like hiding, or drinking yourself into oblivion, you are far too clever to deceive yourself for long . Special years came in the second half of the 1980s, when you were approaching your Saturn return while Uranus, pulling at your sleeve, was urging more freedom. Then in 1994, in case you were not hearing clearly, Pluto began to take charge, prodded by an opposition of Saturn. If intense suspicions, anxiety or confusion muddled the picture, perhaps in a relationship, then you might be tempted to blame someone else. But more likely the doubts about what you really wanted were coming from your own unconscious and it was time to face them. With Pluto square Pluto a few years later some deep cleansing was due, either through settling past mistakes or running away from them. Though that is not a good idea because Pluto never gives up until there is a deal.

1960

This was the start of a decade which would turn lives upside down, leaving society in a state of chaos by its end. It has been called "ten years which shook the world" and, provided you are able to compromise you could be in for an exciting life. But it started with deceptive calm and took a few years for the depth of dissatisfaction to be noticed. This first year was still dominated by conservative attitudes, high productivity and the optimism of an American president, Eisenhower, who said "this will be the most prosperous year in our history". Some of that ambition surely rubbed off on you. But it was an ending as well as a beginning, and about to produce unexpected shocks that disturbed old-fashioned veneers.

With many planets in earth signs you were born to be practical and take authority seriously. But something was seeping into the old control mechanisms as Neptune, the dreamer, now in Scorpio, was about to dissolve worn out structures with its steady drip, drip like water on a stone. In your character this could bring a deep sense of unease if you try to maintain a situation which needs updating. With Saturn inconjunct Uranus you could have fought the system or bought into it so completely that it has become a familiar strait-jacket which you are afraid of losing. Having two such controlling forces at odds with each other means you had to adjust, somehow. Being idealistic as well as practical, and mixing originality and discipline in equal proportions would help. Just don't let one squeeze out the other. If you over-do your conscientiousness you could lose a sense of proportion.

One of the themes in your life will be to "go with the flow" and check old assumptions periodically to bring them up-to-date. This might have struck you as important in 1979 with Saturn, Uranus, Neptune and Pluto, all in the middle of signs and making aspects to your Saturn, begging questions about duty, ambition and authority. And if not then, certainly in the early '90s when Neptune on your Saturn was at the midpoint of Saturn/Uranus causing doubts about institutions you respected. Many were showing their dark sides.

Your year was the beginning of real TV power, bringing information that would change attitudes and turn the world upside down. Early indications that drama was brewing in the US were a sit-in by black students at a lunch counter which set off a series of events throughout the South; the slaughtering of protesters at Sharpeville in South Africa; and the shooting down of an American U-2 spy plane over the USSR. Oil countries formed OPEC to protect their interests against the multi-nationals. In November John F. Kennedy was elected, the youngest US president in history, on a wave of optimism offering new directions for pent-up energy of the early baby boomers. These events surprised traditionalists who expected the old ways to last forever.

An even younger president, Bill Clinton, would experience the full wrath of southern conservatives in the late '90s when Uranus was opposing your Uranus and Saturn opposing your Neptune. That time was your mid-life crisis and could have opened doors to new thinking for you, if they had been shut too tightly.

You were born at the time when old regulations needed re-examining so the best of them could be salvaged and used as a foundation for the future, not a yoke put on you by the past.

1961

This year began the 20-year cycle of the Great Conjunction, Jupiter and Saturn together, which always seems to bring enormous social changes. You were really born into a new lesson of history which seems much clearer in hindsight. Women were still "lady-like" and wore little hats and white gloves encouraged by Jackie Kennedy. But there was an upsurge of youthful energy trying to break through old traditions with new enthusiasm and vision. Anything seemed possible as Yuri Gagarin soared into space, but it was definitely a year of "two steps forward and one backward". The Bay of Pigs fiasco undermined American confidence until Kennedy committed the US to landing a man on the moon. A flood of refugees flowed from East to West this year just before the Berlin wall was built. The wall did not come down until 1989, when Saturn, Uranus and Neptune were all in Capricorn approaching the degree of the Great Conjunction with Jupiter opposite in Cancer. This was half-way through their next 20-year cycle which had begun in Libra in 1981.

Your aims in life may seem ambivalent but the pattern of hidden secrets in your psyche need not be taken personally. With a strong sense of mystery, fantasy or idealism from Chiron in Pisces opposing Pluto and the North Node, and a heightened ambition from Saturn, and possibly Jupiter too, in Capricorn, you could have felt overwhelmed by the rules and wanted to withdraw or have gone through periods of intense rebellion against them. Pity your poor parents and teachers who did not share your urgency to change the future. Fighting your way past authority was something most of you have attempted at some time, and if you relied more on muscle than mind, like the terrorists of your age, you wont have got far. In the early '80s, the meeting of Saturn and Pluto in Libra in a square to the Great Conjunction, could have forced you to accept a bit of cooperation rather than doing everything your way. You will have discovered that putting your head down and bashing your way through only gives you headaches. Instead of pushing over the walls that seem like personal prisons, why not move them a brick at a time and build in more doors and windows.

The Chiron-Pluto opposition and Neptune in Scorpio illustrated dangerous issues involving nuclear power and psychedelic drugs which were still ignored by most people. They also promised an increase of channeled healing and psychic power. You may have felt an unconscious guilt (Pisces) and a longing to escape, or some mysterious power emanating from your Higher Self. Any deceptions, self or otherwise, would be uncovered eventually, and experience would show that facing facts and working things out (Virgo), is preferable to hiding in the dark.

The '90s gave you choices, opening a path to the future. Your Saturn return in 1990 was followed by Uranus breaking up your Saturnian inhibitions and Neptune sweeping them away. A useful year to have restarted your dreams if you found they were a little stale, was 1994 when Uranus and Neptune, planets that only meet every 172 years, were beside your Jupiter-Saturn. The same year, Chiron moved closer to the Earth and opposed Saturn on the axis of your Chiron-Pluto which was a personal opportunity to see any wounds and frustrations that had held you back. Pluto squaring Pluto, made 1997 a time for renewal and to end the century Uranus challenged your Neptune in a waxing square, urging you to leave secrecy behind and enjoy the changes, whatever they were. With your healing power, that was an invitation you cannot refuse.

1962

You were born in a strange year starting with an unusual solar eclipse, involving seven planets in the sign of Aquarius, a hint that you were the strong folks of the future and would demand a lot of personal freedom. This planetary line-up caused panic in remote areas of India as it was thought to be marking the Second Coming or the end of the world! Rather than an ending, you arrived at a beginning. The important aspect of Jupiter and Saturn together was barely over, setting the tone for 20-year cycle of social change. Added emotion came from a Chiron-Pluto opposition being joined by Jupiter, in Pisces. On one hand there was renewed optimism with the Kennedy clan installed in its Camelot; John Glenn circling the Earth; and the first black student being registered at a Mississippi university. On the other, Vietnam was heating up; China invaded Tibet; the stock market was shaky; and the installation of Soviet missiles brought about the Cuban crisis just as we were beginning to believe the worst threats to our peace were over. In hindsight it was a dangerous game of bluff, with complicated secret deals and tests of leadership egos when Kennedy and Khrushchev faced off. It was a nail-biting time.

With that historical background, you have a challenge as well as the heavy-duty tools you need to deal with it. The real weight on your shoulders is to use your power efficiently. Aquarian talents can be usefully disruptive, breaking up worn-out structures to be replaced by more forward-looking ones. But they can also be ruthless if applied too selfishly or impatiently. So much will depend on you finding a balance between the emotional intensity coming from Neptune in Scorpio and the idealistic ideas of Aquarius. One can undermine the other and it is vital that you use discrimination when you play your leadership role — with self-confidence and caring or as a stubborn me-firster. Pity the poor pack which follows you blindly down the nearest sewer just because you tell it to, with authority! Your choice is whether to be a big winner or a big loser as you won't want to stay neutral.

As well as Uranus, the Aquarian ruler, Pluto and Neptune had more worldly influence in your make-up than they do for those who cling to personal problems. That makes your understanding of the pull between inner and outer forces greater than most. It also adds to your responsibility to deal honestly with the complicated ethics of our time since their deeper meaning is obvious to you, if you look. The impulse to overcome trivialities that enslave others could be strong if you sense that your life has a higher purpose.

Pluto and Chiron both deal with hidden sides of character which can erupt like volcanoes whenever they are in need of being cleansed. Following Neptune's urge to withdraw to some soothing occupation gives you opportunities to listen to inner compulsions rather than using logic. But trying to escape entirely would be a mistake.

That solar eclipse was your signature tune. From 1983 to 1984 if you felt slowed down, with Saturn on your Neptune and squaring all those eclipse planets, it was to test your balancing act. Then in 1985 Jupiter went stationary retrograde in the middle of them and you had ample opportunity to check your direction and reset the dial. In 1992, Saturn reached the eclipse point, and your task was to organize long-range plans with the help of clear heads and courageous spirits, making you the "bridge to the 21st century".

By August 1999, another eclipse opposing your natal one, is a test of will power and if you chose the high road rather than a low one, we can all follow with assurance.

1963

Most of you born this year will have a strong awareness of self with Saturn in Aquarius anxious to take action with its waxing square to Neptune. The operative word being "anxious". Neither feeling inferior because you are not perfect, nor superior because other people are not on your wavelength, is going to help. Such doubt could have added to your sense of isolation and prompted you to look after yourself and leave the rest behind. But that is not what you really want. The up-side of being self-conscious is that you take responsibility seriously, knowing that what you do matters. And with Uranus and Pluto in Virgo you do want to be helpful even if you wonder where to direct your initiative. Does it help to realize that you were part of a new chapter for society, being born so soon after the Jupiter-Saturn conjunction. People were becoming aware that something was terribly wrong with how we related to each other and other cultures?

You were born into a seeding period for change and an environment that was becoming more and more unstable as people began to see their world differently, thanks to TV. New leaders were challenging old structures causing anxiety and uncertainty about the new "rules of the game". Many deeply-entrenched traditions which had been taken for granted were about to dissolve. Two oft-quoted slogans of this year — "Ich bin ein Berliner" by President Kennedy in Germany, and "I have a Dream" by Martin Luther King in Washington, placed accountability on the Self. Then the question became what to do about it?

Pluto opposing Chiron was unleashing new levels of criticism and confusion about what is right and what is wrong. Individuals interested in civil rights were joining anti-segregation marches in Alabama and Mississippi and holding teach-ins in New York to discuss Vietnam. Deep feelings of Neptune in Scorpio with Saturn's waxing square to it, were in conflict, and protesters met violent resistance. The need to face past mistakes was accompanied by a fear of going against the tide

For the US, this year started with good feelings but ended in tragedy. Working with optimism and good-will new programs were formed such as the Peace Corps, and Alliance for Progress fueled with youthful energy mobilized by a charismatic president who said "ask not what my country can do for me but what I can do for my country?" A new vision of independence was growing and Martin Luther King led a civil rights march to Washington. Then came the assassination of JFK and Americans mourned a hero who had urged them to change the world. Yours was a memorable year and the beginning of an ethical revolution. The inconjunct between Saturn and Uranus added extra irritation to being self-critical, making this a difficult year to feel confident. As the deceptions became more obvious, public doubts about the use of power would grow, culminating in Watergate in 1972-73 when transiting Saturn and Neptune opposed each other in a square to the position of Uranus this year. By the time you were ready for maturity, in the '90s, a loss of faith in established institutions had reached a high point. Bringing back trust and good faith will be a job for you, which you can do well.

Those born 15 to 20 years before you were preparing to deal with older generations who did not like having their values disturbed. The determination to do just that grew more forceful and became urgent when the century ended with Uranus squaring your Neptune and Saturn opposing it.

1964

This year was unusual, as there were seven eclipses (if you count the one on New Year's Eve) and that means a lot of concentrated energy for you to tap into, when you are ready. Just make sure you aim it in the right direction. As there was a concentration of earth and water influence this year your efforts need patience and careful molding to be productive, otherwise you could get bogged down with anxiety. It was a time when the planets representing new thinking (Uranus) and transformation (Pluto) were coming together, signaling the inevitable destruction of worn-out systems. Being born with a large dose of revolutionary spirit will give you the energy to take a lead through difficult circumstances because of your original ideas. It is your impatience to get into the next century which makes you seem restless and disruptive to anyone who thinks the olden days were the best of times. But your do-or-die spirit, has been heightened no doubt, by a feeling that someone is trying to stop you. Some of your peers, perhaps believing theirs was the only way to right social wrongs, grew into a new breed of terrorists that operated in the '80s, when Saturn and Pluto in Scorpio brought out the shadow side of power-wielding.

Unless you have your feet firmly on the ground you could be too self-sacrificing, or unsure of your own feelings making you easily influenced through criticism. This comes from Chiron opposing Pluto. Chiron, a planetoid, that shows an unconscious vulnerability, was not discovered until 1977, but that just means it lay even deeper in our psyche than it does now. For you it has special significance because by the time it reached your Pluto in 1994 it was closer to the Earth than Saturn making it difficult to ignore. And on the first few days of 2000 it will conjoin Pluto at a degree that squares your opposition. That makes an interesting pattern for you to start a new century.

In the US your year was known as Freedom Summer. Students began to challenge university administrations and join rallies. The struggle for civil rights grew fierce and volunteers registering black voters in the southern states were murdered by the Ku Klux Klan. Music of the Beatles, Bob Dylan and Joan Baez, linked the counter culture, as the flower children, born in the '40s, rebelled with new values and dangerous habits, like experimenting with drugs. And the introduction of the Pill brought new freedom to sex. The slogan of youth this year was "don't trust anyone over 30". An underlying theme for all of you has been to compromise between what you want to do and what you were expected to do by those who were your so-called "elders and betters". The shock of seeing the president's assassination on TV last year, killed the optimism and left behind a feeling that the idealism of Camelot was not real. Your job is to look beyond disappointment and keep hope alive.

Those of you born from the end of last year, through 1968, a period covering the Uranus-Pluto conjunction, something that happens only every 127 years, share an attitude which other generations find hard to understand. By 1995 you will have had a Saturn test, in spades, with Pluto squaring it and transiting Saturn meeting your Chiron opposite that tender spot of Uranus-Pluto. You are here to clean up old politics and use positively the radical changes seeded into this decade. That is an emotional undertaking since you are likely to be opposed by people with entrenched opinions but if you do have the courage of your convictions and can rebel without too much upset you will be doing the world a favor. You did choose to arrive at an emotional time!

1965

Dealing with reality could have been quite a problem for many of you born this year, partly because you may not have liked the reality presented to you yet did not have the means to control your childhood situations. Being the offspring of the "flower children", many of you had a very untraditional upbringing and strange family foundations. With Saturn, Uranus, Pluto, Chiron and the North Node, all in mutable signs, as well as Mars for most of the year, it would not be surprising if you have an escapist side which has left you with some anxiety or fear of disorganization. Take heart, you are the vanguard of a revolution that was exploding around your cradle and which you can sort out with the creative imagination buried deep within you.

This year started a new stage of independence with Uranus and Pluto near their conjunction, something that only happens every 115-127 years, and brings out an intense rebelliousness to anything that is holding back the human need to feel free. But a dose of escapism mixed with anxiety was added by Saturn in Pisces, the opposite sign leaving you uncertain about what to do with your freedom when you got it.

An explosive mix of Mars, Uranus and Pluto left over from last year may have left you with an obsession about action, whether to take it or not. Then an opposition from Saturn, lasting until late May was encouraging many of you born at that time to take wild risks in your late teens. Some of you went too far pushing any envelopes you could find beyond the limits of common sense in a desperate attempt to prove your independence. The positive side of that grouping is your natural resistance to oppression which, when used for the disenfranchised can be of great service. Between 1984 and '87, when Uranus then Saturn squared those positions, was a time for you to hone your tools for action on behalf of the community, rather than just for self. Otherwise you could be among the financial adventurers making or losing fortunes in the '90s, throwing economies out of balance if you equate money with security.

During the year, Jupiter, the planet of expansion, was involved in a solar eclipse and challenged Saturn, Uranus and Pluto. Once again, the question about growth for humanity was how much and how far. Consumerism was on the rise and credit cards were introduced. Everywhere people were growing more restless, impatient with injustice or confused with the new freedoms. The draft for Vietnam increased and race riots and anti-war rallies were seen on TV. Malcolm X was shot and international terrorism was increasing. Then the mini-skirt was introduced and the Summer of Love, which lasted 15 months, was in full-swing in Haight-Ashbury.

It was not a peaceful time to arrive, but since Uranus and Pluto were in the sign of Virgo, just rebelling would not be good enough for you. You needed to replace the rubble left over from the social revolutions with structures that would benefit the mass. Attitudes towards work and productivity would alter radically in your lifetime. As you matured you would be looking for a cause and applying personal discrimination to the kind of changes you thought were needed. Adapting to new ways and being discriminating about them is the theme of your year.

When the combat troops were sent into Vietnam, the year you were born, the longest and most painful American war had started leaving an aftermath of bitterness not yet dispelled. The first Vietnam protesters espoused the theme that "truth will make you free" which is a good motto for your year. After learning about the exposes of Watergate, Iran/Contra, Whitewater and of dirty-tricks in politics and business, digging for truth is a creed you are well able to put into practice. A major eclipse of 1999 squaring your Neptune, while Pluto meets your South Node, brings up questions about ethics, ideals and values, in time for a good clean out of any worn-out weaknesses or confusion. You were born at a time when young professionals, like "bare-foot doctors" and "store-front lawyers", were willing to use their skills unselfishly. Theirs' is a tradition you might want to emulate.

1966

What a year this was. You dropped in at a very mixed up time when old rules were being broken and new political movements were being born. Violent demonstrations overturned governments in every continent and there seemed to be contradictory, yet simultaneous, efforts everywhere to destroy and preserve, with both fanatical rebellion and concern for conservation! These contrasting urges came from Saturn opposing Pluto then Uranus, with strong pulls in diverse directions spreading confusion and anxiety, similar to those for last year. A revolutionary cycle that lasts anywhere from 115 to 127 years was beginning with Uranus and Pluto making three exact conjunctions. Also this year, the long cycle moving humanity from one Age to another (Pisces to Aquarius) was closing with Uranus sextile Neptune offering opportunities to reconsider and tidy up mistakes made since the 1820s. This was a preparation for a new cycle to begin in 1993.

Some aims of the protests may have been pacific but the methods were turbulent with sit-down strikes and bombing. Flowers, beads, peace and love were the hall-marks of the hippie cult which staged, rock concerts, love-ins and happenings liberally mixed with drugs, from the mid-60s on. Rebellion took a destructive path and, while Neptune trined Saturn in Pisces and Jupiter joined in from Cancer, drugs became the easy way of escape. While this emotional stew was lapping around you as a baby, its effect may have been to send you in the other direction, becoming straight-laced. By the time you reached voting age, and Saturn reached your Neptune, at the end of 1984, it seemed you and others born in the early sixties were looking for prosperity rather than change and there was a don't-rock-the-boat attitude. Perhaps you were opposing the fanaticism of your parents.

For many of you, a longing for freedom took you into dangerous situations making you extremists. If "turning on" was easy, turning off was not. As an example of the all-or-nothing syndrome of your year, think of China and its cultural revolution, with young people turning against their elders encouraged by government authorities who were afraid of intellectuals. The Red Guards were brutal, killing 20 to 30 million and eliminating educated people in a mindless rebellion. Not being willing to listen to the experiences of others, young people (your parents' generation) were cut off from the very roots they needed for stability. With long hair, wild clothes and psychedelic music they were showing their confused elders that change was irrevocable. For their parents, born in the '20s and '30s, that was scary as they no longer had control and wondered where they had gone wrong in their children's upbringing. A lot of unexpressed guilt was born in your year.

With Chiron close to Saturn you may have cloaked anxiety with defensiveness, like an armor. By examining your vulnerable points you may find that the attacks you fear are coming from within not from without, making you your own enemy. So sign a peace pact with yourself. Between 1981 and 1998 Chiron, inside Saturn's orbit, should have been easier to identify.

At times you may have been exasperated, or even a bit frightened, at the lack of understanding among authority. Did you feel stranded on a desert island while someone bored holes in the boat you needed to escape? Around 1985-86 it was time to curb any destructive attempts at freedom since Uranus squared the sensitive degree of its conjunction with Pluto and also formed a semi-square with transiting Pluto. By the 1990s you were ready to find your own means of dealing with disappointment when Pluto met your Neptune. Then there was an emphasis on healthy and healthful development. The Virgo and Scorpio influence can give you wonderful healing ability.

1967

The whirlwind of the '60s was speeding up the year you were born, with the conjunction of Uranus and Pluto slowly separating but still in force. It was a time of teetering on the brink with plenty of unrest but not yet quite enough to send us into panic. For the "before and after" it will help to read the descriptions of last year and next year to see the picture more clearly.

The problem of Vietnam was beginning to dominate politics and divide families. Protesters were burning their draft cards and crossing the Canadian border. For Canada it was a year of centennial celebrations and Expo 67, producing a burst of unity and self-confidence that, unfortunately, did not last more than a year or two. This was followed by bitter schisms between English- and French-speaking Canadians still to be resolved. Symbolism that might explain this last flash of joy before facing a dark period could be found in an interesting historical cycle that coincides with your year of birth. It describes the true meaning of the "awakening" connected with the planet Uranus and shows how much we all have to learn about it.

When Uranus was first seen, in 1781, Mars in Sagittarius and Uranus in Gemini opposed each other, forming a T-square to the Sun in Pisces. This conflict of energies suggested that too much enthusiasm could bring disappointments in a fight for freedom. Over-optimism could spoil the dream behind it, until it was adapted to reality. You and your peers may have come to help us wake up to that reality. In the 18th century there were revolutions in the US and France, both of which started with excitement but brought a lot of suffering before there was any victory. Now, more than two hundred years later, some interesting parallels were occurring with Uranus, in Virgo, approaching that T-square pattern. These same two countries were again suffering from internal unrest, and were both destined to be defeated in Vietnam. French troops were replaced by Americans earlier this decade.

When Uranus and Pluto met in 1965-66 they were close to the US Neptune of 1776, and the North Node (point of destiny) of the first French Republic of 1792. For the US, Vietnam brought disappointment and shame which would haunt it into the '90s when your contemporaries would have to experience the Gulf war in a subtle attempt at a military redemption. So perhaps you belong to a generation in whose lifetime the agony and disillusion (Neptune) of nations having to fight for their own liberation will be concluded.

Seeking independence (Uranus) is complicated as it involves responsibility as well as reality and is a lesson about to be learned everywhere. While the student marches and riots were increasing in Europe and North America, African countries were having their own revolutions. Following the "Year of the Generals", in 1966, more coups made this the "Year of the Majors".

Saturn moved into Aries when you were born starting a new cycle of authority. At the time of your Saturn return in 1996 the underlying message for you was to understand, then share, the complex meaning of Uranus.

1968

This was the most turbulent year since WWII and is known as the Year It All Came Apart, which is not the most encouraging title for your year of birth. But this is a case when breakdown led to breakthrough and crises became pivotal in introducing an entirely new world-view. The rumblings of frustration and anger of the earlier '60s were, at last, out in the open and could not be ignored. "Make love not war" was the popular slogan, and that is a pleasanter label for your birth.

Actions of the so-called counter-culture were in full swing. Governments were lagging behind growing public awareness as the television generation came of age having access to international knowledge that their parents were slow to absorb. Starting with the Tet offensive, the US experienced a surge of anti-war sentiment. Military involvement increased in Vietnam and violent battles between police and protesters occurred outside the Democratic Convention in Chicago in full view of a shocked TV audience.

This was a bad year for heroes. Martin Luther King and Robert Kennedy were both assassinated. In Europe, France and Germany were equally chaotic with their urban guerrillas and in Czechoslovakia hope of more freedom was dashed with the horror of Prague Spring.

People born this year had inner contradictions to settle, similar, but more focused, to those facing people born four years earlier and a year or two later. With two difficult inconjuncts, Saturn to Neptune and Saturn to Pluto, there was a lot of adjusting to be done. You were the children of the hippie generation, the rebels against tradition, so it is not surprising that many of you, from childhood on, have been confused about what is normal. What is expected, or acceptable, in your material and moral values has been a mystery. How you relate to yourselves, each other and the society within which you would have to operate is something you have learned by trial and error.

Astrologically you were born into a time when the meaning of freedom, and the many sides of liberation, were about to become an obsession, with Jupiter joining Pluto and Uranus, and Saturn as the apex of a yod with Neptune and Pluto (see 1969). Humanity had plenty to learn about personal wants and needs and how they impacted on a shrinking world. It was time to examine, analyze and prepare to accept that being usefully productive and offering some kind of service was part of life. Developing one's own potential had a purpose, not for endless self-indulgence as a Leo Jupiter may expect, but as a natural way of plugging into a world where individuality meant that everyone had something to offer if only they were given a chance to bloom. That, surely, was the meaning of Thomas Jefferson's inclusion of "the pursuit of happiness" in the requirements of independence. And Bob Dylan sang that if you were going to break the rules you had to be honest about it. Real enjoyment of life and liberty means being a useful individual within a group, doesn't it? At your Saturn return in 1997-98 your yod was reactivated for better or worse, and by 2004, when Jupiter is again in Virgo and Pluto squaring your Uranus-Pluto, with Saturn having its waxing square cautious action could bring you more security, if you need it.

1969

This was a year that gave the world a new perspective — literally. For the first time we got a picture of Earth from space, when men landed on the Moon. And a new view of life down here is what you have come to develop. Life would never be quite the same again, though many of us did not know it then.

You were born into a social upheaval which would not be settled without radical change, started by people born in the '40s and needing to go through several metamorphoses until they, and the rest of us, got it right. Neptune close to its sextile with Pluto, and Saturn still playing yod with Uranus, Neptune and Pluto, were challenging you to bring new spiritual meaning to everyday affairs in a way that would transform attitudes to work, service, loyalty, forgiveness and responsibility. Somewhere in your psyche you have the discrimination, common sense and ability to probe the emotional impulses of people so you understand why they do, or say, what they do. Being aware of the subtle, and often outdated, dynamics of social interaction you can help to change everyday patterns formed from false assumptions and unconscious urges. That is a big task but it needed doing and you are the ones to start it.

The shocks of last year reached a new momentum and this year saw the spread of protests to middle-class, middle-aged North Americans. The anti-Vietnam demos in Washington were so large they had great influence on government. People were waking up to reality with the help of TV news. As more and more kids dropped out of the education system and joined anti-war movements parents were forced to hear their concerns whether they agreed or not. There was too much disruption to be ignored. Young people flocked to Woodstock for a 3-day gorge of music and drugs. A gay-bar was the scene of a riot in New York. Cambodia was bombed and Sharon Tate was murdered by a group high on drugs led by Charles Manson. The shaking up was going to continue but Saturn entering Taurus was urging more common sense. What its yod needed was sensible compromise between escapism and destructive rebellion. Not easy now that it was in a fixed sign.

Your generation can, and may be forced to, find a way out of the trap of earning a living the hard way, with Pluto at the South Node in Virgo. What you choose to be "when you grow up" could be completely different from the options first presented to you. When employment leaves room for imagination it can bring satisfaction rather than slavery. By the time you were ready, the job-market was in confusion and many of you got lost in the shuffle but think of this chaos as a creative step towards a healthier society. Saturn in Taurus is a lesson about resources and values and its irritating aspect from Uranus suggests that there had to be change in job descriptions. Towards the end of the century, circumstances will create opportunities for you to rethink personal priorities in favor of group efforts.. In 1998 Saturn's return to your Saturn was in a waxing square to Neptune, once again in fixed signs, a time for grounding dreams and taking active responsibility on behalf of the environment

1970

If you read 1969 you might find this year is more of the same but with emphasis on a renewed search for meaning as Neptune changed signs. This was the year the microchip was developed, a perfect symbol for the universal exchange of news that would eventually bring out truth, as well as spreading confusion! Deep emotions had been buried too long and it was time to know about, then share, more of the world's suffering.

From this year forward, reliance on honest leadership was wearing thin, with good cause. The FBI were spying on citizens and the national guard shot students at Kent State University. It was the end of Utopian dreams and the beginning of the "sobering '70s", years when the public was presented with unpleasant glimpses of the misuse of authority — like Watergate. Suspicion of government, the press and many institutions would grow until it turned to cynicism by the '90s. One of your roles will be to use your Taurus Saturn to re-establish some stability for the next century, restore trust by separating the real from the phony. In 1999, around your Saturn return in a waxing square to Uranus, economic struggles could break up old patterns and, with Chiron completing its stay in Scorpio soon to join Pluto in Sagittarius, unexpected action in international finance is likely.

Cracks in our social fabric were appearing all over the place the year you were born. Uranus moved into Libra shaking up old partnerships and the Beatles broke up, then as Neptune entered Sagittarius, Jimi Hendrix and Janis Joplin died from drug overdoses, as, sadly, many of their fans would do in the years ahead. But there were a few bright spots. When Apollo 13 got into trouble, the Soviets offered to help, a nice gesture from an old enemy.

From now on any dreams for an ideal society would require hard work and patience to make them real. Women's lib marched in New York; over 100,000 protesters joined forces in Northern Ireland; and Earth Day, in London, drew the largest demonstration in history. People are never at their best when they are frightened and while the level of fear was rising good will was being eroded. Hidden anger took different forms with the increase of hijacking, kidnapping and violence. In Canada, the kidnapping of a British official, then the murder of a Quebec politician, plus a threat of armed insurrection brought out the army, which was a terrible shock to a peace-loving country.

Leaving the emotional sign of Scorpio, Neptune plunged into a more escapist mode which would keep gamblers happy for a few years until they saw the futility in anticipating easy-fixes. Saturn in Taurus is prone to economic pessimism until it feels stabilized but it also insists on reality. Altogether you, and people born shortly after you, were being presented with the task of rehabilitating social goodwill, starting around 1995 when loss of faith in institutions was at its height. That was a time when Uranus was in harmony with your Pluto and Neptune at the same time, inclining you towards some serious rethinking about how to make the most of your special gifts. By then intelligent opinion was losing faith in public behavior and began calling for less violence in "entertainment", while the escapists grew wilder and wilder. A mass sobering up had begun and your ideas could be in tune with it.

Finding your place in a chaotic society where jobs were melting and equality seemed lost would not be easy. But in the late '90s you were ripe for change, especially if you were ready for a spiritual experience when Pluto was on your Neptune.

1971

The slow planets, Pluto, Neptune and Saturn all changed signs, ready for new exposures of duplicity. With Neptune (illusion) and Jupiter in Sagittarius, the sign of expansion, this was an easy year to be fooled by false optimism. The antidote to that falsity was a natural urge to develop psychic ability, which many of you have done. When Saturn opposed, as it did in the second half of the year, it was more difficult for the less sensitive to maintain faith. But that is exactly what you, and those born in neighboring years are here to do. For another 14 years the fog of Neptune invited self-delusion or serious spiritual growth. Take your pick!

This year was the half-way point of a Saturn-Neptune cycle, which started in 1952, in Libra, bringing lessons about who to trust, who is deceptive and who deserves forgiveness. This opposition had the effect of separating the dreamers from the realists. When unpleasant news emerged such as the political facts contained in the Pentagon papers; evidence of a massacre by the US army at My Lai; or Idi Amin's brutal use of power in Uganda, some took it seriously and others preferred to stay in cuckoo-land. The Shah of Iran gave a lavish party in the desert to celebrate his importance just a few years before he was overthrown! The cycle ended in 1989 when the truth about Russia, East Berlin and other former "enemies" was due to emerge giving another chance to review reality. Too much dreaming confused the financial world. After several bank crises and the busiest day ever, so far, for the New York stock market, the American dollar was devalued.

There is something of the happy gambler about the Sagittarius influence that needs to be treated with caution so that it does not lead to outright dishonesty as it did among powerful circles in your year of birth. It is a reminder to build your life on rock, not the sand of unreality. Your role is to be sensitive to misinformation and to search for the truth.

In the US, national loyalty was under stress with news reports from Vietnam. In your lifetime, probably before the end of the century, the nation will be questioning its values and facing its former use of power in embarrassing situations. This is when your slogan can be "truth will set you free". You can lead the way to forgiving those who have learned the hard way and want to start again. And there will be many.

This year saw a new low for freedom and an increase of secrecy by the White House. President Nixon and his administration misled the public with secret bombings of Cambodia and the compiling of an enemy list designed to harass journalists and politicians who opposed him.

Pluto would spend the next 13 years, in Libra, breaking up relationships which were decaying, and slowly unearthing injustices, before it went into its own sign and really dug up the dirt. This left many of you with shaky family structures and having to experiment with your own loyalties and affections. After another 12 years of Pluto in Scorpio, which certainly tested your (and everybody else's) ability to draw sensible limits in relationships, the pain could recede. By the late '90s even Hollywood was introducing a few happy endings interspersed among its usual blood-lust. When you find something and someone to believe in (and you can if you look in the right places) without getting fanatical about it, your Saturn return in the year 2000 could be a joyful time.

1972

Here goes another year when reality (Saturn) and fantasy Neptune) were at either end of a teeter-totter, bringing up truth, or continuing deception. Examples of that were Vietnam then Watergate. Suspicions about true facts of the war were surfacing, and burglars attempted to steal political material to influence a presidential election. Therein lies the moral for you — who to trust? Like last year's curriculum you will find that truth is safer than fiction and you cannot believe everything you hear.

The on-and-off again effect of these two energies can be very confusing if you do not know what, or who, is being honest. Always keep an open mind and look at both sides of any situation. Having lived through an era when lack of knowledge was a real draw-back, now a confused public was being deluged with too much. As the tidal wave of the Internet swept over us in the late '90s rumor became dangerous so you will have to keep a clear head and search diligently.

You could have experienced a test of your values early in your teen years. Around the age of 13 or 14 Neptune was ready to fool you if you were not being realistic after it had moved over your Jupiter and squared your Pluto. There was lots of optimism then. In 1985 Jupiter was in Aquarius, the sign ruled by Uranus, and Uranus in Sagittarius, the sign ruled by Jupiter. There was joy in generosity and massive rock concerts collected money to aid starving Ethiopians. By 1986, Saturn was making its first opposition to your Saturn, challenging your dealings with authority and bursting a few balloons. That could have been a lonely or anxious experience. Thinking back to that time would make sense of two other crucial periods for you, in 1995 and 1997, when Pluto was pulling up any over-heated dreams as it moved across your Neptune and opposed your Saturn. If you dealt with the first test seriously, you were probably in the right groove for the others, and able to slide through them happily.

Unless you were well motivated, you could have experienced difficulties in education as many schools were succumbing to the influence of gangs in your time. If peer pressure is hard to resist ask for advice. Having an older and wiser mentor always helps during sticky patches in life even if you cannot accept their whole opinion your mind can be stimulated to see another angle. Eventually, your age-group will need to deal with traditions and ancient wisdoms by taking the best of the old and marrying them to modern situations, without getting frustrated and throwing them all away.

It was a year of new visions that would experience ups and downs. Joint agreements did not always work out but were steps forward such as the Great Lakes cleanup, grain deals with Russia, peace proposals to North Vietnam, talks with China.. The Dow Jones average broke through 1,000, and the space shuttle program began, which, if you remember, had a disaster in 1986. Reaction and replanning of the stock market, space travel, UFOs or new views of the Universe will come in your adulthood, so it is an exciting time to be alive. Just remember to check, and double-check, before arriving at conclusions.

1973

People born this year and next have emotional experiences to deal with that are far more symbolic than just personal suffering. Neptune had reached a point of opposition with the rare conjunction of Neptune and Pluto of 1891-2. That in itself is significant but, if you live in North America it has other dimensions because that conjunction was exactly on the US Uranus, as well as a sensitive point in Canada's chart. Like others born in this decade you have come at a very special time.

Many of you will feel bewildered for any number of reasons. Even as early as 1982, your world may have seemed chaotic with the Great Conjunction of Jupiter and Saturn close to your Pluto, and Uranus on your Neptune. Your first lesson in philosophy may be to understand that chaos has its usefulness. Authorities in your early life were often confused so you may often feel adrift, without precise direction. You have, if you look for it, the faith to swim to calmer waters.

Another unusual grouping when you were born was Neptune conjunct the two asteroids, Ceres and Juno, which are concerned with intimacy and security. This could give you expectations of closeness which turn out to be disappointing because of lack of realism surrounding you — yours, a parent's, or a partner's. The exciting side of that combination is psychic sensitivity. Learning to trust instincts rather than wishful-thinking is very important for you.

When deeply entrenched structures need to be changed the wrecking crew makes an awful mess. Well, you arrived to welcome it. In fact, you probably joined it, not so much as a rebel but as a spectator who gets pulled in to assist. Painful though the process may be if you try to hold on to the past, the object is to dissolve old values and put better ones in their place. That means that your life is a search for self-worth based on new values to replace out-dated ones.

Before the end of the century Pluto reached the position of your Neptune, ready to root out excessive dreams, and all set to tune into the Pisces search for universal love on an international scale. This requires discrimination. Making choices between compassion vs. charity, creativity vs. escapism; a belief in human goodness vs. the ugliness of drugs and pornography, were all tests to be faced as the 2,000 years of Pisces merged into the Aquarian Age. Of course, you were not taking this test alone, but with so much planetary help you could lead the way.

Symbols of changing times were appearing in the heavens. A satellite photographed Jupiter; the first US space station, Skylab, went into orbit; and astronauts took a space walk. On Earth, deception and misunderstanding, associated with Neptune, was causing havoc while the waning square of Saturn to Pluto brought power plays into view, such as confrontation between native people and military forces at Wounded Knee; the overthrow of Chile's president in suspicious circumstances; and political lies uncovered at the Watergate inquiries. Neptune represents oil and this year brought energy crises and line-ups at gas stations because of erratic supplies. The devastation of nature by oil spills and the Gulf war turned many in your age group into environmentalists.

Your trip is a crisis of faith, but don't panic. A good time for action is 2012 with Saturn squaring your Uranus, and Pluto squaring Pluto. Then the North Node conjunct your Neptune and Uranus in a nice trine give opportunities to resurrect trust in each other.

1974

Patterns made by the slow planets were getting more and more complicated as if they were pushing us all into shape. Pluto, particularly, with its waning square from Saturn, was reminding that sooner or later reality has to be faced just as Richard Nixon was being pushed into acknowledging his misuse of presidential power. As it was in Libra, Pluto was setting up a lesson about cooperation showing the futility of making unreasonable demands on relationships, personal or social, and how dreams could become exaggerated.

With an insecure Saturn in Cancer, inconjunct Neptune, as well as square Pluto, yours is a generation which would have to learn not to be dependent — on partners, on government, perhaps even on justice. Crazy gambling, emotional escapism, or reliance on hand-outs, was definitely not the way to succeed then, or now. With Jupiter and Neptune in each other's signs realism was in short supply so if you do have grandiose dreams it would be smart to step back and imagine the consequences both positive and negative. Example — Patty Hearst, daughter of a millionaire joined the terrorists after being kidnapped, leading her into miserable years ahead.

Like last year, this was a half-way mark for an important test of the meaning of the American Dream, started more than 80 years ago. The promise of success to anyone willing to gamble may have brought immense wealth to a few greedy seekers but often at other people's expense. Thomas Jefferson's idea of the "Pursuit of happiness" in the Declaration of Independence was more spiritual than financial and something for everyone, not just the few. As Neptune has now come to the opposition of the degree of that conjunction of Pluto and Neptune on top of the US Uranus (in 1891-92), a review of social values, and particularly the symbolism of Neptune, was coming due. You are here to introduce different attitudes to the energy of all three planets in time for the new century.

A better balance in society is what Pluto in Libra was aiming at this year. Urban devastation caused by inequalities was becoming more visible all over the world and rising oil prices and interest rates showed how fast stability can be undermined. Finding difficulty in earning a living, as many of you will at some time, could puncture any fantasies of streets paved with gold for some while others are left in the gutter.

A positive side of your psyche is the capacity for spirituality. An important meaning of Neptune is faith and an understanding that human beings are not in complete control. Relying too much on personal will while ignoring the mysterious forces and synchronicities can throw humanity out of balance. If you think about it, that could be something you well understand. Keeping your feet on earth while letting spirit soar is a difficult exercise but one you can understand, then teach, with your Neptune and North Node in Sagittarius. When you find a belief system which satisfies your search for a better world you could discover creative ways to bring that American dream alive in a new way. In the year 2001-2, when Saturn, the builder, will be on that 1891-2 degree, and opposite your Neptune, both you and the US will have ample opportunity to restructure attitudes to independence.

1975

This was certainly a pivotal year with two waning squares. After the build-up of tension during the last few years, important social changes were taking place (Jupiter in a waning square to Saturn), although it would be a long time before some of them were noticed. If you were born this year you are certainly no shrinking violet, with Uranus in Scorpio most of the time and several slow planets in cardinal signs, but you do need to be ready to parlay with the enemy rather than burst into flame, symbolically. In your lifetime endings and beginnings will abound and if you are a futurist you will enjoy the immense changes promised. A course in crisis management would be a useful addition to your education.

It has been cited as the year the industrial age ended and the information age began. New technology was rampant with answering machines, pocket calculators, digital watches, VCRs and video games, all ready to blow our minds. And emphasizing the confrontations of the year, the world heavy-weight championship, between Mohammed Ali and Joe Frazier, was held in Manila, on a day appropriate for a fight among the Greatest! Sun and Pluto were conjunct, Saturn in a waning square with Uranus and the Moon was in Leo. It was broadcast by satellite TV the world over, for the first time. There was an air of brinkmanship about this year, with that social pair, Jupiter and Saturn, in a conflict that requires a conscious acceptance of facts before taking new action. By the end of the year the planet of independence, Uranus, changed signs, and squared its "opposite number", Saturn. Both squares demanded an adjustment to reality, which is the theme of your year.

Around your 21st birthday, it was appropriate to review your vocational goals, to keep on the right path. Being born in a year of dramatic breakthroughs, as you were, moving forward is important to you and it would have helped if you were able to recognize your direction early. With transiting Uranus going from Capricorn into Aquarius by 1996, filling the fourth quarter of your T-square, your way ahead should have been visible by then. Otherwise, if you are avoiding reality, that could have been a restless or frustrating time. Last year and this saw the worst recession for nearly 40 years but problems, especially economic ones, were becoming global. "We are all in it together" will eventually become apparent, so will "We have seen the enemy and it is us". Even in the rush of doing-your-own-thing individuals were slowly waking up to accepting personal responsibilities and seeing their problems in a more universal context. Being a year of sudden change from the disruptive to the progressive, your message is to take initiative after careful consideration of facts and emotions involved.

Crises abounded. Unemployment hit new highs from the effect of exorbitant oil prices, then after the infamous terrorist, Carlos, broke into an OPEC meeting, and kidnapped the delegates, prices changed! New York city was on the brink of bankruptcy. American troops evacuated Vietnam. A president was forced to resign over his dishonesty. International Women's Year put the spotlight on the "gentler" sex which was not prepared to be submissive any longer. Having been burning bras for a decade, groups reached out in a more business-like way to each other around the world.

The lesson from now on is to use personal potential positively and for the common good. That is sound advice for all ages, but definitely for you.

1976

Another year of endings and beginnings brought in a bunch of souls ready to tackle some deep-seated problems involving power and power-sharing. Last year was disturbing and, in many ways, this one was even more extreme. The social atmosphere surrounding your tender years was full of anxiety but being born this year certainly does not condemn you to being unhappy. Far from it. You have the determination to heal some deep-seated hurts and transform them into exciting new opportunities.

As last year's description shows, the world was changing fast and that was extremely upsetting to most people. By the time you shoulder your own authority society might still be turbulent but at least it will be used to change.

This year was the start of punk, with its unfettered actions and aggressive attitude making it a difficult trend for traditional society to understand, let alone handle. With so much disruption coming from youth born in the late '50s and early '60s it is no wonder that normal people were frightened. Protests had become acceptable but the raw hatred of this new counter-culture was something else. The year also saw a peak in a cycle of terrorism that lasted from 1968 to 1979 as Saturn and Uranus complete their fight started in 1942, at the last degree of Taurus.

The grouping of Pluto at the midpoint of Saturn and Neptune prompts an obsessive denial of emotion, and can lead to depression or a fanatic desire to escape from the rules. The message here is "don't be impulsive." Punk was saying "there is no room for me in your society". And that is not a path to happiness — or peace.

In your adulthood you will recognize you were born at a watershed and are strong enough to weather the shocks. With two massive earthquakes, and the first signs of a flesh-eating disease, Ebola, nature showed the need for some destruction before an equilibrium was achieved. There was a lot of looking back for the United States, with its bicentennial celebrations but all was not joyful when the unnerving stories of Vietnam vets were heard. In China, Chairman Mao died bringing an end to the 10-year horror of his cultural revolution. And in South Africa the violence of police reaction to riots in Soweto, seen on TV, outraged the world. All were important turning points.

Deep in your psyche, if you dig for it, you will know that the punk demolition going on was just shock treatment that would clear a way for the building of a more spiritual approach to life with your Sagittarian Neptune. By the year 2000 be sure to search for a belief system that means something to you.

Other important years were around 1997 when Saturn opposed your Pluto, a warning that you are more likely to get what you want if you cooperate instead of pushing. At the same time Mars and Saturn were giving a similar message in their long drawn-out face off from Libra to Aries. It was a time of two steps forward and one back with peace-keeping efforts being frustrated by exploding anger and impatient outbursts from those needing help. Then from 2010-12 when Uranus is opposing your Pluto, the new age could be taking shape in a much healthier society if your Scorpio energy has been well utilized.

1977

The same tension from Pluto that caused last year's anxiety was still in place so you too, have to overcome a tendency to harbor pessimism. Help was on the way, though, when something new appeared on the cosmic calendar in November. Chiron, a planetoid, asteroid or comet, (astronomers seem uncertain which it is) was discovered. It is thought to be the "rainbow bridge" between the energies of Saturn and Uranus which had squared each other the previous year, suggesting that it was time for stubborn egos to come to terms with each other and start cooperating instead of fighting. Saturn conflicting with Uranus in a waning square is a reality check about stubbornness. Denial takes over if the ego refuses to let go of old ideas. And that makes it difficult to stay in sync with natural timing, like the "universe unfolding as it should"! By dealing with the responsibility that Saturn demands, a new freedom can be gained through Uranus, which is the lesson for you.

With Pluto and the North Node together in Libra, this was a great year for relating in a new way — with equality. If you get that right you could be the diplomats of the future. The flip side of that combination is an excess of anger leading to violent confrontations. So watch out for extremism, either yours or those around you. Your role is to take the sting out of altercations then heal the rifts.

Humanity needed a signpost and Chiron was it, a hint that the path from the old to the new can be smooth with a bit of effort once the source of deeply-buried pain or weakness has been faced. Its position in a birthchart is a significant point that must not be ignored, like an Achilles heel or a sliver that irritates until it is removed. Then the wound can heal. For most of the year it was in Taurus, suggesting that values and resources were subjects for new consideration.

A first step in the healing of our planet is rebalancing the earth's poles, symbolically at least, and that means calming any extreme ideas or emotions that lead to blind or destructive passions. Before it was sighted Chiron, in the sign of Aries since 1969, was calling for initiative, and going into Taurus its search for new values began. You have been born at the start of a universal lesson in sharing. There are sufficient resources on our planet to provide sustenance for all, so why do people starve? Good question, and knowing this you can assist with redistribution. Some healing of old wounds will be needed before the new age settles in comfortably but the passage into a readjusted universe should be easier than most people are making it. Knowing this, you can help others see it for themselves.

It was an unusual year from the start with nature illustrating how dangerous imbalance could be. A Pacific current called El Nino brought the coldest winter in recorded history, then droughts, floods and fires. That current would do the same again many times in the years ahead, specially in the '90s, when weather patterns around the world went berserk. You have an important part to play in restoring balance so keep an open mind for clues as to how and where. In 1999, a waxing square of Saturn and Uranus calls for action, and you need to be ready.

1978

Coming between two extremely interesting years, as you did, your role is to tidy up the old and begin the new. All the slow planets were making waning aspects ready to close long cycles and start anew before you reached 16. Jupiter was sextile Saturn; Saturn sextile Uranus, and semi-square Pluto, approaching a square to Neptune; Uranus semi-sextile Neptune; and Neptune sextile Pluto. You could not have a bigger hint than that.

The emphasis for many of you will be on finding a faith and direction that helps to understand the inner truth of humanity's search for spiritual satisfaction with Neptune in the philosophical sign of Sagittarius and its ruler Jupiter rushing through three signs, from Gemini to Leo. Yours is the generation that is preparing for a new crusade, looking at social mistakes made in the past and ensuring that they will not be repeated in the same destructive way, hurting those who are powerless. Before that lesson is learned, no doubt, dramatic evidence will be available before the end of the century, catching you in your late teens when most of the slow planets start making waxing aspects. Then next year, with the once-in-a-half-millennium shift of Pluto, new seed packets were ready to be opened. Being in the middle you need to bring the past and the future together by living firmly in the present.

With Chiron now on the heavenly map, and in Taurus, an awareness of the need to deal with the negative side of materialism's destructive waste had arrived. In time you could have been leading the clean-up crews as Chiron conjoined your Pluto in 1996 when both planets are at their nearest point to earth. Taking those first vital steps in changing values and having the faith to do it are the big tests for you.

Interesting things happened to money the year you were born. New York nearly went bankrupt, just saved by the Fed; the price of gold peaked; then Wall Street had its worst week in history, up to that time. All were hints that something about calculating wealth and worth had to be reconsidered, both personally and universally. The picture comes clearer when you think of money as natural energy. When people hoard, either through greed or anxiety, the natural flow of resources is dammed up, causing symbolic droughts and floods which eventually hurt everybody. Nature accentuated that message in the late '90s when El Nino brought havoc to all continents.

Uranus in Scorpio at the mid-point of Neptune/Pluto was about to change the scenes of medicine and religion, and test the dark side of unregulated freedom. Ancient knowledge was being brought to light but so were new diseases. Spirituality was increasing but religious fervor was becoming dangerous. A tragedy of this year occurred in Guyana, where a religious group led by a fanatic, Jim Jones, committed mass suicide and/or murder, depending on who believed in him and who was forced into death en masse.

Finding that thin line between no belief and too much dependence on easy answers is your difficult task. Many will lose their way on that particular tight-rope, so take warning and clear out obsessions and empty dreams by 2002, when Pluto crosses your Neptune.

1979

This year began with a very significant change in the heavens when Pluto, usually the most distant planet astrologers track, moved inside the orbit of Neptune and was closer to the Earth. It only makes this shift once every 250 years and stays there for 20 years. So you, and those who will be born between now and the end of the century, are well-qualified to help humanity understand Pluto's dangerous energies. And they can be dangerous until they are taken seriously. An ultimate test against corruption, Pluto presents some "black and white" choices about the use of power, and as you mature you will have important decisions to make about how to deal with the cruelty of Man's (and woman's) shadow side. Many of your contemporaries will be living in societies enraged from fear or frustration, with people of all ages turning violent. Apart from the usual crime and hooliganism, group action, from schoolyard bullying and swarming to international terrorism and ethnic cleansing has continued to increase. By the time Pluto moved into the excessive sign of Sagittarius in 1996, road rage and anger in all forms of abuse was effecting normal life as misdirected passion emerges like lava from a volcano.

When you were born the slow planets interlocking with each other in waning aspects were closing cosmic cycles started in the '40s and '50s after the building of the Bomb. This leaves you free to open a new chapter of use, or misuse, of power. Pluto bearing the seeds of the future was at the midpoint of

Saturn (the builder) and Uranus (change). At the same time Uranus lay between Neptune (dissolution) and Pluto (destruction) challenging the degree of the momentous Uranus/Pluto conjunction of 1963-65 which brought an intense fight for freedom still going on. But a cry for REALITY was growing louder.

With Saturn having such a workout, and meeting the North Node in Virgo, old attitudes to charity (Pisces) needed reexamining. Some positive criticism and acceptance of responsibility was urgent. Demands for hand-outs would not save those addicted to dependency and the idea of serving had to become more practical than emotional. Drawing those lines may seem hard-hearted, but it is not helpful to overload the lifeboat. With your common sense, in 2003, when Pluto reaches your Neptune, and by 2008 at your Saturn return, this should be apparent.

Politically many changes were attempted in the '60s but not all of them were successful. Reviewing their methods and intentions to construct or destroy will show you how to heal social problems. If we need examples of shifting power, there were many this year. The US opened diplomatic relations with China; leaders of Israel and Egypt signed a peace treaty; Margaret Thatcher was elected British prime minister; the Shah of Iran went into exile and US embassy staff were taken hostage; Mecca was invaded by hundreds of armed men; and a bishop was massacred on the cathedral steps in El Salvador. Then a dangerous mistake occurred, in Pennsylvania, when a leak (Neptune) occurred in the atomic plant (Pluto) at Three-Mile Island.

Universal attitudes and values were being tested on many levels helping the conscious evolution of humanity to catch up with the historical time-table, moving from one Age to another. From this year onward, the pressure to consider ethics (Pisces) increased as the sophistication of technology (Aquarius) accelerated.

If all this sounds complicated to your parents it probably makes sense to you as the language of astrology will be a natural means of understanding self and nature by the time you mature. It is literally time to clear away out-dated structures so that modern ideas can take their place.

1980

A lot that was happening last year spilled over into your year to remind the world that it was time to turn on important corner. The slow planets were gradually massing ready for unusual and radical changes. Uranus was at the mid-point of Neptune and Pluto, a time to expect a sudden change leading to an emotional transformation. Nature's answer to this mix was the rumbling of the volcano inside Mt. St. Helens giving a warning before its eruption. Then later, adding to the message that something was radically wrong, AIDS was becoming disquieting news.

This year was bringing a strong message that "honesty is the best policy", with Saturn in a waning square to Neptune. The older you grow the more obvious it will become that deceiving others always rebounds on oneself.

Knowing that "you can't fool all the people all of the time", your generation can help straighten out the confusion created when authorities try to keep secrets. Dirty deeds committed at this time came to light by the end of the decade when the two planets conjoined in Capricorn, the karmic sign. One such event, known as the October Surprise, was the apparent behind-the-scenes conspiracy to use hostages in Iran for political advantage in the American election. It worked for the moment, but when facts emerged years later they smeared the careers of high officials in a government already under suspicion. An appropriate theme for your year was the release of the "Empire Strikes Back", the second of the Star Wars trilogy, illustrating that action leads to reaction.

At the end of the year, the two planets representing social growth, Jupiter and Saturn, came together in Libra, ending their 20-year cycle. It was a time of preparation for better teamwork to bring justice between people and organizations. But first an old cycle had to be completed. Where did all the idealistic "store-front lawyers" and "bare-foot doctors" of the '60s go?

With Jupiter in Virgo, and Saturn there until October, you will experience some anxiety over work, too much or too little, eventually forcing a more cooperative approach. "Time share" and "flex time" would solve many employment problems. When you mature, in 2009, with your Saturn return, the old ways of working will seem out-moded.

This was the start of a "decade of greed" which saw the gradual decline of morals that would leave many social problems for you to clear up as the century ends. But with strong help from the cosmos, and all the slow planets, you have plenty of backing. You were ready to mature fast around 1993, when Neptune and Uranus together, squared your natal Pluto. New ideas and new values were being born out of a genuine search for truth started by your Uranus/ Neptune/ Pluto combination. If you were appalled at the ethics of adults at such an early age, that could have been the push you needed to realize that you were more advanced, spiritually, than they and were born to do some serious teaching. So stick with your beliefs.

You are in good company as souls coming along behind you are well prepared to help, too. Though not responsible for getting into an ethical mess, you are well able to get out of it.

1981

January launched one of those 20-year cycles of the conjunction of Saturn and Jupiter associated with the deaths of US presidents, and known as the "curse of Tippecanoe". The Great Conjunction, as it is called, has the effect of causing turbulence in space, literally, when the winds of Jupiter upset the stability of Saturn. In astrological terms it means that the current rules of society are due for a change and those born during this time would be ready to start them.

The changes you will experience before your 20th birthday, the next conjunction, will focus on Libra matters, relating, partnerships, peace. You qualify as definite peaceniks with a mandate to reach out to others and negotiate. Saturn in Libra shows responsibility to deal fairly, and Jupiter there increases your wish to join forces in teams rather than going it alone. Also this year, Jupiter met Pluto, adding to your power to negotiate, or increasing your use of violence, the shadow side of Libra. The choice is yours.

The conjunction occurred three times during the year and an eclipse in Aquarius coincided with a violent Mars square Uranus, presaging danger to world leaders. A month later President Reagan was shot, then in May the Pope was shot. In October Anwar Sadat was assassinated. This particular conjunction interrupted a theme that has been operating for 150 years, and seen as a curse against American leaders by the Indian, Chief Tippecanoe, so the story goes. If you believe in synchronicity, rather than curses, consider this. Up to now, the conjunction has been in an earth sign (Taurus, Virgo or Capricorn) but this time was in an air sign (Libra). Earth being associated with solid form, represents a body, but air is intelligence, and instead of the president's body, the target of this year's curse was the president's mind! Which could explain why after President Reagan was shot, but not killed, he was suspected of having mental problems and eventually developed Alzheimers.

The cosmos does produce timely symbols. A dramatic warning of dangers ahead came from a mysterious source in Yugoslavia, when children claiming to see the Virgin Mary, brought the "Miracle of Medjugarje" to world attention. In your teens, devastation in that country was caused by power-mad dictators inciting ethnic stubbornness. Once again, ruin resulted from turning one side against the other

The next Great Conjunction, in 2000, back in earth once more, for the last time, is also proceeded in 1999, by a dangerous eclipse in Leo, exactly opposite the 1981 degree, with Mars again squaring Uranus. This is also likely to be a year that anger and negative energy can be dangerous. Accompanying the conjunction in May 2000, Mars in Gemini opposes Pluto, rife for a war of words, needing all the diplomatic abilities you can muster. In your role of heralds of peaceful cooperation and honest communication, you had a timely arrival and are very welcome. At this time the attitudes of superpowers were anything but peaceful. The year started the biggest arms build-up in history, an unnecessary expenditure which left the Soviet Union bankrupt and the US with unused aircraft carriers, fancy space weapons and large tax increases. All because both sides were convinced the other one was the enemy. A lesson you have come to teach is that differences in culture, race or ideas cannot be bridged by force. As the comic book said, "we have seen the enemy and it is us".

1982

An exceptionally significant year, yours was a time of an extraordinary focus known as the Jupiter Effect. All the planets from Mars to Pluto were gathered within an angle of 72 degrees, between Libra and Sagittarius. Having that kind of concentration in your chart should make it easy for you to tune in to your purpose and stick with it.

Sagittarius is a sign that reaches out on a universal scale and by the time Jupiter and Uranus get together in Aries, in 2010, you could be prepared to take charge with new initiatives for global cooperation. Altering values on a world scale will be your job. There is nothing petty about Jupiter-Uranus!

1984

At last, George Orwell's "dreaded" year of Big Brother had arrived. It started with the planets of fantasy and expansion — Neptune and Jupiter — moving hand-in-hand into the karmic sign of Capricorn, just as Saturn and Uranus would do five years later. Capricorn settles the score by demanding acknowledgment, and often payment, for past indiscretions. And with Pluto ensconced in Scorpio, this began painful times for anyone with skeletons in their closets, which sometimes took years and years to emerge.

Being born this year makes you aware of the effect of action on reaction and you will be wise to proceed with caution. The most important message for you is to tiptoe through the tulips and avoid anger or violence like the plague because what you initiate comes back like a boomerang. Symbolism tells that story. There was a forceful combination of planets in January and July when Saturn, at the mid-point of Mars/Pluto, was holding the lid on a boiling pot. Then Uranus, rattled the cages as it met the mid-points of Mars/Jupiter, and Jupiter/Saturn, adding extra tension. Altogether it was a high energy time for action and anger.

Assassinations, hijacks, strikes, storms, earthquakes, collisions and air crashes, brought an over-dose of drama that, in retrospect, left an ennui that deadened the senses. And that could be a block to your feelings unless you are encouraged to express them gently. A Pluto and Neptune warning of hidden putrescence in society and its organizations came with a deadly gas leak in India. Both planets changed signs this year, always a hint of a need to retune awareness and adopt new attitudes.

Perhaps more to the point of Orwell's plot, Pluto settled into its own sign, Scorpio, where the effects of concentrated power would be unearthed, eventually. Big Brother was not yet conspicuous but was busy collecting the details of our lives by encouraging wider use of credit cards, ID and computer print-outs. Privacy was becoming a thing of the past as hackers learned how to invade computerized data but the general public would not bother about the danger until much later. By the time Neptune left Capricorn, in 1998, trust in governments and officialdom had disintegrated as a result of Pluto's exposures of corruption in previously respected institutions.

Most of you born this year who respond positively to Neptune's psychic energy have a very useful talent. The ability to see through lies gives you a chance to identify the real idealists and to avoid being conned by the phony.

Pluto was going to continue digging out the dirt until the worlds of finance, politics and sex were cleansed, even if it took decades. By 1996, when it entered Sagittarius, old cases of abuse and wrongful convictions were being brought to light. Then when it reaches Capricorn, in 2008, the time to settle karmic debts will have arrived.

This year brings an opening round for stronger spiritual reaction to the easy-come-easy-go approach of the immediate past. It was time to get serious about "man's inhumanity to man." Those born in winter, spring and fall have both Saturn and Pluto, the planets of control, in Scorpio, giving extra responsibility for handling power wisely. You are all part of a generation of healers in many senses of the word, with plenty of common sense mixed with your mystical side.

1985

The year you were born was a tough one but no more than many still to come. Tensions were building as the slow planets gathered at several crucial midpoints that need careful handling, but one rare combination was a real bonus for you. Jupiter in Aquarius was in Uranus' sign while Uranus in Sagittarius was in Jupiter's sign. That combination, known as a mutual reception, linked the mental plants together in way that promises an enthusiastic search for wisdom. In esoteric astrology, Jupiter rules Aquarius, so all in all, you were well prepared for the positive changes in thinking and communicating that were ahead. All this makes you able to understand the times of crises to come and wise enough to see the path through them, once you have reached maturity. So you are a valuable addition to our bid for progress.

With Pluto moving closer to the Earth, as it has been doing since 1979, its difficult energy would be specially pronounced for the next 14 years, boosting emotional intensity guaranteed to test everyone's ability to withstand temptations. You could have experienced unusual pressures in your childhood growing up while society was struggling with Pluto's lesson. But it also means that, when the next century begins, you can be right up front leading your peers through its violence and obsessions and out the other side when Pluto is on your Uranus and Uranus on your Jupiter. That is an equation that adds up to a deep understanding of what ails the less enlightened. By working to integrate your own need for freedom (Uranus) and search for wisdom (Jupiter) early in your life you can have confidence in your principles while the world in general is confused.

You arrived in a year of disasters so your appearance with the planetary strength you brought with you was very timely. When you use it to communal advantage there is less danger of getting swept into the raging floods of violence and corruption of the years ahead. Dramatic events were increasing in this "worst year in the history of aviation" with 1,500 people killed in crashes; AIDS, first noticed in 1979, was causing panic; Terry Anderson, the US journalist, was taken hostage in Lebanon; a cruise ship, Achille Lauro, was hijacked by terrorists in the Mediterranean and a Greenpeace boat protesting French nuclear experiments was blown up in New Zealand — to name a few.

On the positive side, the world was becoming more concerned over racial tensions and starvation in Africa. Bishop Tutu and Jesse Jackson, the American activist, were drawing attention to apartheid, and journalists were writing about the disastrous drought in Ethiopia. In the summer a spectacular rock concert in London, called Live Aid, raised millions of dollars to feed the starving. On the other hand, the US Congress voted millions for aid to the contras in Nicaragua, and Oliver North was beavering away in the White House basement secretly buying and selling illegal arms for Iran.

This was the International Year of Youth, though adults at the time were growing more and more confused about how to deal with the wild energies transmitted by the music scene. As you grow older you will be able to see the deep divisions between people willing to accept reality and those holding too tightly to their old ideas about control, like Ollie North for example! Your prominent Jupiter was making a waxing square to dominating Pluto, offering you the opportunity to redress the balance of power using both heart and mind. That is the badge of an idealist with common sense.

1986

Striving for independence must be high on your agenda with your Sagittarius Uranus so active. When you were born it was about to square the degrees of Virgo in which its dramatic conjunctions with Pluto took place in the mid-60s. Uranus is also forming a transiting semi-square to Pluto in Scorpio this year. Uranus disrupts and Pluto plants new seeds, for better or worse. Merging these two energies is one of the most important tasks of this century and that is a priority for you and others who arrived in surrounding years. Your parents' generation were born into a social turmoil of protests and craziness that shook up the traditionalists. It was the start of a global revolution to give the humble (Virgo) a chance to inherit the earth, but not to destroy it. The '60s marked the coming of age of the Boomers, whose challenge was to learn how to restructure power, with their Saturn conjunct Pluto in Leo. Now it is your task to carry the revolution into chapter two.

When the planet representing the urge for freedom met the emotional intensity of Pluto it is not surprising that humanity went wild, and if the children born into the '60s maelstrom apply tough discipline to their own children it is to protect them from their parents' mistakes. As next in line you have a powerful inheritance. But be patient in developing your own God-given individuality. If you postpone your rebellion until you are wise enough to be diplomatic you will understand that although fundamental change frightens people it can be positive rather than destructive. What matters is how it happens. By 1999, with Pluto on your Saturn in Sagittarius, a few hints of your role could have emerged.

Your year started with a ray of hope when the new Soviet leader, Mikhail Gorbachev, announced his wish for nuclear disarmament, but that was quickly followed by the ghastly shock of the Challenger explosion, then three months later by the nuclear melt-down in Chernobyl. Both tragedies symbolize the emotional results of scientific mistakes, with Uranus at the mid-point of Saturn/Neptune, and the disappointments of unrealistic dreams, of Saturn slipping between Neptune and Pluto. Such combinations of the slow planets brought attention to the downside of pushing too hard, too fast for independence. The excitement and upsets of last year with its growing terrorism and suspicions of conspiracy were continued, and political visions (Uranus in Sagittarius) and faith in leaders (Neptune in Capricorn) were changing, both pro and con. With Gorbachev's program of glasnost (openness) letting in the light and the US president's involvement in the Iran/Contra scandal revealing a dark side, you can see that nobody is all "good guy" or "bad guy". You have options of practicing strong principles and being more, or less, open about them. If you choose less be prepared for Pluto to bring out the dirt in the new century when it transits your Saturn.

The social awareness of your Jupiter in Pisces, forming a waxing square to Saturn then Uranus, could direct your idealism to new ideas well-rooted in sound spiritual aims. These will be tested out in 2016 at your Saturn return with a waning square to Neptune on your Jupiter. By then society may have learned the benefit of behaving ethically rather than deceptively. Your good fortune could depend on searching for some belief system without falling into any Pluto trap of fanaticism. The early years of the new century bring Pluto to your Uranus, a cue for an exciting change of goal for you if you are ready.

1987

The cosmos was advertising the importance of this year by sending a supernova in February and a "lunar standstill" in September, when the Moon reaches its highest declination in a cycle lasting 18.6 years. Both events were drawing attention to space beyond our control. A supernova is an explosion of a star that is running out of energy and the last one was seen in 1604. This one was the Blue Star prophesied by Hopi Indians, the Peaceful People, as being the final warning for our mistreated planet to avoid destruction. They had recognized this century as being the time of a kill-or-cure conflict between materialism and spiritual awakening and had tried, unsuccessfully, to share their beliefs with international leaders since 1914.

Adding to the symbolism of endings, in August the mathematics of many ancient cultures coincided for the Harmonic Convergence, and many people around the world held ceremonies to demonstrate the need for spiritual cleansing before it was too late. As if to underline the unusual times, the slow planets were making strange patterns with each other. Uranus between Saturn/Neptune, was continuing the apprehensions of the last two years; and transits of Pluto and Neptune formed a semi-square, their first major aspect since their conjunction of 1891-92, repeating the call to take seriously a need for renewal of morality. That conjunction at 8 degrees of Gemini was a hallmark of our human evolution for this century and this year Saturn in Sagittarius opposed its degree, an aspect giving time to reflect on how best to build new foundations. Neptune, now settled in Capricorn, the sign demanding reality, held promises of opportunities for redemption and transformation through faith and a change of values. Jupiter, Saturn and Uranus in fire signs most of the year added energy to personal efforts for increasing awareness.

What a year to be born! It was a time of broken records and contradictions when it seemed that luck and retribution went hand in hand. In the first three months the Dow Jones average rose 3,000 points before the stock market faltered then crashed on Black Monday in October. Excessive greed and yuppiedom were being exposed with Leona Hemsley, the multi-millionaire hotel owner, jailed over taxation and the insider-trading of Ivan Boersky and junk bond swindles of Michael Milken coming to light. So were the shocking revelations of presidential lying in the Iran/Contra hearings, far more impeachable than Bill Clinton's weaknesses. Terrorist activities of the IRA increased and in the US a "holy war" broke out between TV evangelists over the Jim and Tammy Bakker scandals. But all was not negative. The cold war was receding as Mikhail Gorbechev shook hands with the public lining Washington's streets.

Sad notes this year were the enormous quilt displayed in Washington to remind the public of the spread of AIDS, the modern plague; and a rash of teenage suicides, with transiting Neptune squaring the position of Pluto in the early '70s, bursting obsessive dreams. Neptune's desire to escape was leading to more drugs and a wish to "stop the world I want to get off". Its reality check for you will come in the first few years of the new century when Pluto joins your Saturn and opposes that conjunction of a hundred years ago, and Neptune reaches a waxing square to your Pluto bringing actions to test your values. Being born in a year that requires such karmic choices should be exciting, and satisfying, once you see them clearly and are ready to "keep the faith baby."

1988

This was the year that Pluto in Scorpio came closest to the Earth at 0 degree declination in September reminding us earthlings about the need for transformation and the "death and resurrection" of old habits so that our direction can move from destruction to construction. The dangers of extremes were being brought to our attention, hammering home the Orwellian message that society was decaying. Pluto's role is two-sided, either to corrupt or to resist corruption and that is a choice that will be made very clear to your generation. To explain the problem more clearly, the symbols of the past and future, Saturn and Uranus, came together this year at the last degree of Sagittarius. Then, simultaneously, they moved into Capricorn while Pluto was stationary retrograde, another reminder to take seriously the need to clean out traditions that were limiting growth so that wider vision could be substituted. Moving backwards, they repeated their meeting at the same place, with the Sun opposite, later in the year. Their conjunctions make your year both an end to unlimited optimism and a beginning of a more sober approach to world problems. You came in for Act 1 scene 1.

You were very young when your Pluto had important challenges. Uranus made a waxing square to it in 1998 and Saturn opposed it the following year, those were times to take life seriously, as you will be able to understand later, when you can look back. Oppositions are opportunities to see yourself as others see you so hold up the mirror and look. Again, in 2003, your Pluto is under duress from Neptune in Aquarius squaring it. Waxing aspects are good times to move forward, but from fixed signs, as they are here, action requires much thought as it can land you in a log-jam if it is motivated by obstinacy rather than resolution. Good intentions are paramount in this case. That year too, Saturn is opposing your Saturn-Uranus conjunction adding tension to your stop-and-go urges unless you can be flexible. Being both cooperative and firm sound like contradictions unless you are particularly careful when choosing your team. By 2007 and 2008 Pluto arriving at your Saturn-Uranus conjunction and moving into Capricorn, could be extremely helpful if you have been living with your own brand of glasnost. That is when basement doors could be flung open to let the sunshine in.

The pull between the freedom (Uranus) to expand, and the rigidity (Saturn) to maintain the status quo was about to widen the year you were born, separating those who wear rose-colored glasses from the realists. The cosmos does not pull its punches and from this year onwards the choices between holding on to the past or challenging out-dated regulations were becoming obvious, but some of us are slow to respond. Later in your lifetime the need to question authority and expect sensible answers should be clear.

Pluto is not letting anyone off the hook now it is so close to the earth. Violence in Ireland and Israel escalated in March and floods, fires, earthquakes, explosions and hijackings came day after day throughout the year. Then in December, when the Sun reached that last degree of Sagittarius, squaring the position of March's solar eclipse, a plane exploded over Lockerbie, illuminating the danger of ambivalence. Its political implications were too hidden and too complicated for us to understand the why's and wherefore's then, but the anger of a Pluto in Scorpio was taking its toll. The opposite of anger is healing and making Pluto your friend early in life will save you a lot of heartache.

1989

This year the planets' messages were very clear. Blend spiritual awareness (Neptune) with responsibility (Saturn), or else.... Up to now there had been time to contemplate, think, dream even play with the intuitive, psychic, Christ-like abilities within us, but this year was a kick to "get on with it", seriously. Saturn, Uranus and Neptune were all in Capricorn and opposed by Jupiter in Cancer and a very strong Pluto was in Scorpio. They spelled out your task as being to work with a mixture of earth and water — material and emotions. That means washing away old structures to prepare the ground for future changes.

The mud they make is the means of molding something different. So think of yourself as a potter with the freedom to plan new shapes in whatever area of your chart they reside.

You have a variety of components to use. Pluto's clamor for a clean-up was stronger than ever in September when it reached its closest point to the Sun (perihelion) in its 250 year cycle. Saturn and Uranus were together last year but this year, in Capricorn, their union is a more practical matter. The Earth was ready to move! On the surface Neptune energy slides and slips as the fog rolls in but underneath it can dissolve foundations with the force of a subterranean tidal wave. With Saturn the symbolism means heaven and earth, so there is opportunity to capture Neptune's will-o-the-wisp character and make sense of the intangible yearnings for improving the world down here. This was the year the space probe Voyageur 2 was close enough to Neptune to send back photographs. A neat hint of Saturn's ability to zero in and frame this mysterious object.

So now we have seen it, what's next? Being the ruler of the Pisces Age, Neptune represents a belief system, a faith that if we play our part the universe will encourage us. That faith was about to be tested before humanity could move on to the cerebral energy of Aquarius. We have to prove to ourselves that we are prepared to "let go and let God, as Shirley MacLaine had to do on her self-discovery trip to Peru when she drove down a mountain without touching the steering wheel!

Then there was the emotion of Jupiter moving into Cancer in August, with the nurturing instinct to hoarde or share the basics of life support. This was a year to redress imbalance and it called for an interesting switch. The shape-shifting required new rules from now on. Those who had taken responsibilities seriously were ready to be taught to rely on divine guidance. And those who lived in the dream-world of dependency had to be prepared to shoulder their share of the burdens.

This year's many dramatic headlines spelled out a story of change. In February and March massive oil (Neptune) spills off the coasts of California and Alaska were only two of thousands of others that occurred in this Neptunian year. Oil was due to become a less popular commodity. In June the world watched the confusion of Tiannanmen Square when a bid for freedom (Uranus) exploded and was curbed, for the time being. In November came the "Fall of the Wall", when Germany opened its borders and knocked down the barrier between east and west. Each of these events seeded radical change which took time to manifest. Late in the '90s Saturn in Aries stirred up activity of the Capricorn-Cancer aspects and Uranus squared Pluto, but perhaps the full effect of the change of direction will not be obvious until after 2012 when Pluto in Capricorn, Uranus in Aries, Saturn in Libra and Jupiter in Taurus complete the chess game.

1990

Unsettled could be the adjective for those born this year. If "home is where the heart is" you might be doing a lot of moving before your foundations feel firm enough. And settling down is exactly what most of you want to do. The shocks that ended last year led into a serious period of tension when efforts to dominate were swinging between a search for security and a refusal to give up by those in charge. Governments were "tightening screws" as situations were slipping out of control.

Jupiter, the planet of expansion was particularly busy challenging rebellion, confusion and authority as it made its oppositions to Uranus, Neptune and Saturn. In the sign of Cancer the effect was emotional and being accompanied by Chiron, its desire for protection came with a defensiveness as a reaction to unconscious fears. Planets in the sign of Cancer want to drop an anchor and build a shell, hoping to be nurtured wherever they happen to be. But Chiron there punctures the optimism of Jupiter and opens up doubts about the future. It needs a great deal of affection to compensate. The oppositions cause suspicion that the enemy is strong and the "Barbarians are at the door". The overall task of those born this year will be to find a balance between panic and faith through serious consideration of reality.

The best characteristics of Cancer and Capricorn represent the right mix of nurturing and disciplining, kindness and maturity, which makes for healthy growth. When you get them working together they produce ideal parents. But your own parents may have been feeling tensions about their goals and control. Society was presenting them with schisms, which led to stress, between having families or careers.

It was a year of displacement. In many countries people were fleeing or being forced from their own homes, while others were being allowed to return after a long period away. American and British hostages in Lebanon were released and Iraqi troops left Iran after eight years of war. In the Balkans and in East Germany, for different reasons, refugees were moving backwards and forwards and violence was growing out of panic, anger and frustration. The president of Iraq, Saddam Hussein, was repositioning himself for another thrust for power and in August miscalculated American response when he marched his troops into Kuwait.

With Saturn, Uranus and Neptune in Capricorn, ecological and monetary crises were vying with political struggles, setting themes for the rest of the decade. Nature, with tornadoes and earthquakes, was upsetting old weather patterns and would grow even more violent in years to come. Japan's stock market dropped suddenly shaking confidence and destabilizing the global economy. These sudden changes show that coping with extremes without losing your balance will be something that you will need to work at. When Saturn completes its cycle, in 2019, it will be close to Pluto testing your will power and common sense. Your earthy planets are capable of keeping your feet on the ground, however shaky it is.

1991

This year saw many political upheavals. It started with a strange war in the Gulf over oil distribution. Watching the surgical precision of bombing and the constant discussions on TV, the audience was brought into the forum, to watch the lions fight — the old order against the new. The opposition of Jupiter and Saturn in fixed signs showed this was not a war that could be won. Leaders of the old and new worlds need to work out a compromise to coexist. With Uranus (change) and Neptune (oil) approaching their 172-year conjunction, coming up in 1993, this was a hint that future supplies and prices could be unreliable.

For a more personal meaning, Uranus and Neptune in Capricorn herald a spiritual upheaval bringing tests to assure that those with earthly authority are working in harmony with the laws of the Higher Self. In other words, we should be responding to the soul urge for greater awareness of the goodness in human nature. With the planets of the Universal Mind (Uranus) and Universal Love (Neptune) in the sign of the initiate, your beliefs are important. Where religious authorities have become rigid there is need for change and acceptance of differences.

In your first decade, power struggles on many levels — political, scientific and religious — were about to play themselves out in ways that were painful but transforming. Ecological regulations as well as events surrounding laws and governments were being judged harshly, perhaps on an other-worldly level! Humanity will be called to account for its mistakes in those areas.

This is yet another year of initiation for your parents. Those born from 1968 to 1974 when Uranus was in Libra were spiritual harbingers of the peace and love so desperately needed on our ailing Earth. And these are their testing years. As you mature you will be able to look back, as will others around the same age, at the pressures and temptations parents were under as they dealt with their own inner development. If they had the courage to oppose the decline of morality and set themselves and family high standards, they need applause. Their growing consciousness can be an example for you. Society was about change and some people have to lead the way, but that is not easy.

Irritations in marriages were increasing, perhaps helping you, eventually, to see that partnerships need equality if they are to last. To avoid disappointments in love, and there were many at this time, it would be wise to examine the lines of control. Who is manipulating whom? Cooperation will feel more natural for those born in the last couple of months of the year, when Jupiter went into Libra.

In the United States, election year brought the entrenched minds up against the restless new thinkers. Little had changed since the oldest president, Ronald Reagan had been succeeded by vice-president, George Bush, with the same group of advisers. Another generation was about to take over. Bill Clinton, the youngest president ever elected, and his youthful team were not welcomed by Washingtonians. Being willing to adjust to new needs is a major test for you as it was for them.

This was a dramatic time. A coup in Moscow led to the dissolution of the USSR. Ethnic cleansing of the Balkans was being ignored by too many other countries, hoping it would not spread. But it did. The conclusion for you will be to face difficulties before they get out of control. When Neptune goes into Aquarius, over your Saturn, in 1999, attitudes may have changed around you, or within you, even at that early age. At the time of your Saturn return in 2021, it might help to find out what happened then.

Traditional structures of government, justice and medicine are being forced to keep up-to-date. Alternative health systems already flourishing will be accepted as normal by the time you grow up. To build a firm base for the future changes in child care and education will be priorities for any new group in charge, and you could be the early beneficiaries.

1992

Old regimes and traditions were being shaken up as Saturn and Uranus worked together in each other's sign, in a mutual reception. And the transition brought confusion, deceit and dirty tricks, with Neptune also in Capricorn. The limelight was on Capricorn, the karmic sign, which brings its tests and initiations. In the Ageless Wisdom, of Alice Bailey, it is the gateway to a higher evolution for those willing to accept the responsibilities of maturity. From now on authority will be shifting from top down hierarchy to a community of shared efforts and talents. Material values have to give way to spiritual ones either through choice or coercion. This is the change required for humanity to progress and tests will come in many forms. Boomerangs coming back have to be accepted as lessons learned on the path leading to World Service which is the soul aim of our planet.

The results of past treatment of our mother Earth, will become glaringly obvious in your lifetime. Before it can nourish all people a new balance between the giving and taking of natural resources will have to be found. Protests and violence in many countries continued throughout the year as did nature's protests through snow, floods, and tornadoes, taking their toll on every continent.

This was not a year of high morality and those born this year, and in years ahead will be aware that ethics have to change if we are to survive. The mountain top of Capricorn gives a good view of the mistakes and triumphs of past generations so you will have lots of examples to avoid, or to follow.

Events that stand out as bad examples were the race riots following the police brutality in the Rodney King incident; the sexual orgy at an airforce celebration known as Tailhook; and the "dirty tricks" ads of a presidential campaign. A civil war raged in Serbia. A different kind of confrontation ended wisely in separation after unhappy scandals of Charles and Di. The good examples may be more subtle and mystical. An astronaut, Edgar Mitchell, affected by his view of the Earth from space became aware of an interconnectedness of the universe. To answer such questions as "who are we, how did we get here and where are we going?" he founded the Noetic institute to explore the links between science, spirituality and consciousness and to remind us that each individual affects the universe as a whole. This year a conference in Washington probed the anomalies of scientific and psychic phenomena and put a stamp of respectability on the research of many unexplained mysteries. Official cooperation of great minds working with reality and sensitivity is a good theme for the coming conjunction of Uranus (mind) and Neptune (feeling) with the scientific background of Capricorn.

An experiment in community sharing was the signing of North American Free Trade Agreement by the US, Canada and Mexico. The year ended with the election of a young president, a future reminder to those born now, that this was a year when new visions were coming into consciousness.

By 2014-15 when Uranus is squaring your Uranus and Saturn meets your Pluto, deep emotions mixed with restlessness could lead you to reshape your directions to harmonize with your soul purpose. That will be a time for reflection and faith, with Neptune opposing your Jupiter.

1993

People born this year, and this decade, will face the drastic choices that Uranus-Neptune bring. As agents of old ways attempt to undermine the new shapes of organizations, many traditional institutions will appear to be wobbling. In Washington, the year started with celebration and new optimism as the first of the Baby Boomers was inaugurated as the youngest president. Bill Clinton with his entourage of excited youth, swept into the Whitehouse with Hollywood aplomb and current music. But with Uranus and Neptune about to conjoin in Capricorn, the sign of government, and Chiron on Leo opposing an Aquarian Saturn their dreams for the future were going to meet a few brick walls and undergo some changes. The old guard and inexperience held back the wave of hope for political reform, temporarily. As pioneers, Bill and his friends were in for a bumpy ride and many learning experiences.

Chiron in Leo, opposing Saturn, is an invitation to break through traditional barriers by developing a will that allows for self-judgment, but it also promotes divisions. As resistance from Saturn was growing stronger, the picture for you born at this time is to keep moving forward while treating authority with respect and checking your knowledge. In other words avoid rigid thinking and condemning without solid proof.

The gap between people and leaders was widening as both facts and gossip were leaving both sides frustrated. The new American regime elected to make changes was resisted from the beginning by established powers. Hints of scandal and secrecy were rousing public suspicions and in many countries voters were losing faith in elected, and non-elected, powers as past mistakes were revealed. The destruction of a cult in Waco; a new trial over police brutality in the Rodney King incident and the flooding of the Mississippi brought shocks and urgent demands on those in charge. One step towards conciliation saw the leaders of Israel and the Palestine Liberation Organization together for reluctant handshakes on the White House lawn.

The dream-breaker of Uranus-Neptune shows an attempt to change the ideals of government, but on a more personal level, it is a warning to keep your goals rooted in reality and bring the spiritual and material into harmony. While Uranus in Capricorn wants to rebuild with new architecture, Neptune was weakening out-of-date structures. The best of this conjunction, which only occurs about every 172 years, brings upsets which adjust old values and eventually strengthen faith. Although this was a divisive time it also produced an upsurge of interest in esoteric lessons preparing ground for new visions. There was plenty of encouragement for those ready to progress.

It was a year for the Ageless Wisdom to effect more people with its teachings and its Great Invocation. In Washington, the Center for Visionary Leadership was discussing and promoting stronger ethical values, while in California the New World Servers continued to reach out globally with their full-moon meditations.

By the end of the century the rulers of two Ages Pisces and Aquarius were in Aquarius ready to establish new elements of camaraderie by accepting differences as strength. Your Saturn return, in 2022, lands Pluto on your Uranus-Neptune conjunction, ready to test your willingness to evolve. But you do not need to wait until then.

1994

A recurring theme this year is the interplay of Chiron in Virgo and Saturn in Pisces, the wounded worker feeling victimized. For much of the year they are opposite, causing tension between self-doubt and confusion, wondering who is in charge, or who should be in charge? By August Chiron getting closer to the Sun moved inside the orbit of Saturn, and stayed there until 1998. Like a spiritual doctor doing a house call, Chiron brings a new focus on old wounds, offering a prescription for healing any past hurts that are preventing growth.

As a bridge between the structures of Saturn and the explosions of Uranus, Chiron's link is to assure change while respecting the status quo. But being caught up in Saturn's domain, as it is, it requires effort to push forward with the brakes on. Uranus itself is in Saturn's sign delaying the move towards the future still further. This adds up to a frustrating year and its lesson could be to progress at a sensible pace not too fast, but not too slow either, without losing sight of your goal to put something right, even if that seems difficult.

Saturn itself is semi-square to Neptune, the first important aspect since their conjunction in 1989, when many new dreams were being envisioned. This year they were being tested and the problems were beginning to show, especially in Europe where countries liberated from the confines of a strict system were experiencing disillusion.

There is still another message from Saturn. Continuing a theme about teamwork started in 1982 when it conjoined Pluto in Libra, these planets made their first square this year, which is a time to renew future plans without rushing into things. It is that old "go slow" warning when it comes to relating. Denial of your own needs for someone else can be dangerous. Any serious partnership requires careful building and that does not happen overnight.

With so much influence from Saturn, Pluto and Chiron, you have a serious role in restructuring society. That requires discrimination and caring, even as early as 2008 when Saturn will be on your Chiron opposite Uranus on your Saturn. That could be a time to consider apprenticing for some craft supplied by sensible Chiron. A serious hobby could turn out to be a lifetime's enjoyment if you train patiently.

The year ended with Jupiter and Pluto together, an emotional mix that gives healing power to those who would use it wisely. Keeping the ego out of the way by standing back for an objective view is the best way to overcome impatience and frustration. And listen to other people who might have ideas and inspiration, before making up your own mind.

With Pluto at the end of its own sign, you have a role of spring cleaner, shaking out any moth and dust of corruption. Around 2023, at your Saturn return, Pluto will be ready to leave Capricorn after its long test of organized authority and much of the cleaning may be finished. Thanks to you.

1995

Sign changes of two slow planets this year give you a good mix of all four elements, once Uranus moves out of earthy Capricorn into airy Aquarius. Pluto flirted with fire in the first three months and the last two as it dipped in and out of Sagittarius ending its 11-year purge of watery Scorpio which brought so many long-lost secrets to the surface. Painful though that has been for many, the cleaning process was necessary and is only this thorough every 250 years when Pluto is in its own sign. Between April and November the opportunities for a final look into the underworld, gives those born this year the opportunity to delve deeply into your own psyche and heal any pain you find there.

The planets of responsibility (Saturn) and sensitivity (Neptune) are in each other's sign, in a mutual reception, which means they can work together even though their urges are so different. They can either bring anxiety and confusion or serious attempts to develop spirituality. As the millennium comes to an end, surrounded by increased violence, distrust and shaky economics, many people were turning inward for answers.

In the US, the surface optimism of a Sagittarian Ascendant was about to be replaced, painfully, by a deeper wisdom when Pluto reached there and opposed natal Uranus, in 1998. As Pluto slowly approached the Ascendant darker forces of the country were being revealed showing the weaknesses of the independence with which it was born. Humanity seemed to be taking two steps forward and one back in understanding the responsibilities of liberty. The mass gathering of colored men in Washington for the Million Man March, excluding women and other races, was a doubtful help in healing divisions. The bombing of a federal building in Oklahoma, feats of the Unibomber, the alarming growth of para-military organizations, and the domination of drugs and greed were all symptoms of sick societies.

With Jupiter in a waning square to Saturn, it was a year for social reality and greater efforts towards bridging racial and cultural gaps, not the time to lose faith in spite of its disasters. An individual's values can effect communities positively or negatively as shown in the collapse of a nation's finances in the "Mexican meltdown", and the selfishness of one man in the Barings Bank failure. Then in September, when Chiron entered Libra, another agreement signed between Israelis and the Palestinians caused the assassination a few weeks later of the Israeli Prime Minister, Yitzhak Rabin. In Canada a referendum to resist separation won by only one vote. A peace treaty was signed between the US and Vietnam closing 30 years of misunderstandings that started with Saturn in Pisces opposite the Uranus-Pluto and ended with Saturn's return.

In 2020, Saturn and Pluto will be together over your Neptune, for a serious review of your beliefs and ethics. That could mold your authority with decisive choices to take the high or low road, using either deep compassion or ruthless deception. In its call to strengthen the powers of goodness every vote counts. As this is something you are here to do your considered opinion will be valuable.

1996

This was a "fasten your seat-belts" year with the cosmos determined to get our attention. From the moment it began the year looked serious, with five planets in Capricorn and Jupiter joining in two days later. In the next week Uranus, back in its own sign as mythical Prometheus ready to steal the fire of the gods, was sending a strong wake-up call.

By February, Chiron in Libra, the centaur who rescued Prometheus from his pain, so the story goes, moved as close to the Sun and Earth as possible, setting the scene for some essential lessons in cooperation right here below. Earth itself was moving into a photon belt of high energy that would require a lot of physical and mental adjustments for us all.

The first of two comets arrived coinciding with important messages that needed attention. Hyakutake appeared in March, close to the earth for the first time in thousands of years, maybe even as long ago as the era of Atlantis. Not far behind, the other comet appears next year.

As if all this was not enough to digest, in September a very unusual pattern was formed with trines, sextiles and squares linked in a mystical rectangle and grand fire trine. Yet another message to take all opportunities to embrace a higher spiritual level. With the opposition of Chiron and Saturn, a theme of the year was to turn confrontation into cooperation and avoid the polarizing of extremes. Let's get back into balance.

Those of you born this year have no excuse for ignorance or bigotry as the world's problems grow clearer. The time for learning at our own speed is past. The Hubble space telescope has begun showing masses of galaxies extending its views far beyond our solar system and realization is dawning that following our own will may not be the right path. A little humility is needed and those capable of moving to a higher level of consciousness are leaving others behind

One clear Chiron lesson about the dangers of divisiveness came when the trial of O.J. Simpson started, and justice was manipulated for months by racial discrimination. Communication technology (Uranus in Aquarius) created a mass audience on TV giving the public a window on a flawed judicial system, the symbol of a wounded Libra.

With Jupiter in Capricorn squaring Chiron and later, Saturn, you have a responsibility to tackle prejudice once you become aware of its destructive nature. That, with the fire/air sextile of Uranus and Pluto, offers a means of opening minds to the benefits of social justice. Events in your life will continue to give clearer views of the need to improve ethics and morality. Being blessed with a mystical rectangle, adjusting and helping others to adjust is your theme.

In 2018, Chiron starts a new cycle in Aries just when Uranus is squaring your Uranus. That could be the first step into new mental territory as a keen warrior, or the divine Fool ready for adventures.

1997

As a year of sudden excitement and shock, with emotional highs and lows, those born this year should remember to ignore extremes and look for a middle path in life. This was a year of headlines and drama and has been called the Year the World Caught Fire. That is as much a metaphorical title as literal but there were more forests burned around the world than any in recorded history. The astrological combination that fits such an inferno would be Saturn and Pluto moving into fire signs and linked at their midpoint by reckless Uranus, joined by Jupiter, at the hazardous degree of six degrees Aquarius. Fire signs are warm and exciting and added to air signs can spark a conflagration, as they did this year and can easily get out of control, as any fire-fighter will tell you.

As well as fire there was flood. Lots of it. In Canada, the city of Winnipeg was surrounded by the raging of the Red River which inspired a national rally to help the victims. Fire, floods and tornadoes as Acts of God, bring mass upheavals but the combined effect can bring extraordinary endurance and courage. The weird weather patterns were blamed on El Nino, a cold current in the Pacific ocean named after the Christ child, as they had been in 1977.

Chiron had a role to play as the "inner teacher" for those ready to learn. It made two waning squares, crises of reality, to Neptune then to Uranus. That puts those born this year on notice to consider any tendency towards reckless escapism that could cause regrets. Ill-considered actions may have long-term effect, so it is best to think twice before leaping.

Warnings to limit expectations with realism were numerous. Neptune in Capricorn, joined by Jupiter in January, expanded unreal ambitions and illusions would hit new highs. Several dramas this year would show how fallible, or misleading, authorities can be. The outrageous fraud of Bre-X, a Canadian company, shocked the country when shares sold on false information about a gold strike rose to dizzy heights only to be found worthless six weeks later. The level of denial was increasing rapidly as Saturn approached the square of Neptune before it left the sign of karma, next year.

Another example of denial came when the long trial of O.J. Simpson ended with a not guilty verdict that few people believed was just. In spring a comet arrived that was last seen from earth nearly 2,500 years ago, now called Hale-Bopp. It triggered strange beliefs among the superstitious (Pluto in Saggitarius) and members of a cult, the Heaven's Gate, decided to join the comet, by committing suicide as a group.

Drama erupted in high places with President Clinton starting his second term hounded by more scandal which would lead to an impeachment trial. And Princess Diana, recently divorced, was killed in an auto accident. The world went into mourning with its illusions of a fairy-tale princess. Then four days later it lost a more earthy saint, with the death of Mother Teresa.

This was not a happy year but the upsets had a positive side, challenging fantasy and displacing many who were resisting change. By 2020, Saturn and Pluto will be together in Capricorn, squaring their last conjunction in Libra in 1982. Then in 2026, Pluto at that sensitive six degrees of Aquarius will be with Saturn and Neptune, completing their dance started in 1989. Again and again the message about reality and imagination has been repeated for you.

1998

Saturn and Neptune, the planets of plans and imagination and how to use them, changed signs this year, giving you plenty of choice. They were in a waxing square first from Capricorn to Aries, then again from Aquarius to Taurus. Waxing squares are for action, so you are here to put some of your dreams into shape. But Saturn in Aries tends to hold back afraid to stick its neck out and, in Taurus, wonders whether it can afford them. Be patient. When your visions are in tune with the Universe they will work. The fixed sign square does have negative possibilities though, if stubbornness gets in the way of vision.

Jupiter in Pisces adds a further level to your castles in the air and an urge to believe in angels. Wonderful. But be warned. If your wishes are not well-founded they may be as difficult to control as hot-air balloons on a windy day. That means be realistic as well as spiritual. From March, a waxing square of Jupiter to Pluto, added even more illusion and a rise in religiosity based on obsession rather than tranquil belief. That is something you might meet in your teens when Neptune is in Pisces. When these planets come together at the beginning of Aries in 2026 be sure to have your dreams lined up ready to go.

Pisces can lead you to expect too much and many people got hurt this year driven by schemes to get-rich-quick. Promises that sound too good to be true, probably are. Another danger comes from obsession with gambling, bingo or the stock market. In time you will be able to see how shallow materialism is as a measure of success.

As Neptune settles into Aquarius, the soul needs a higher goal and an aim to serve a community in which we all have a place. The world is now too small for individuals to flourish without regard for fellow-man.

You were born into dangerous times. Racial extremists were gaining ground with bombs and violence, widening divisions instead of negotiating with good will. The many attacks by White Supremacists, the terrorist attacks on American embassies in Kenya and Sudan and retaliation by the US airforce, do not promote the peace and universal love, the world needs so badly.

Pluto's obsessions were activated by a square from a solar eclipse in Pisces. First India, then Pakistan, exploded nuclear bombs, which was not the wisest way to use its Saggitarian power. The ruthless methods used by lawyers and politicians against a self-destructive, Bill Clinton, were other examples of overkill.

Listing the mistakes of the year is gloomy, with quarreling nations, and disasters, natural and otherwise, growing more dramatic. But a positive side of this is a reminder to pull together, not apart. Such misery is a powerful lesson of what has gone wrong, and with your active squares of Jupiter to Pluto and Saturn to Neptune your energy can lead you away from similar mistakes.

In 2015 Saturn, at its waning square to Neptune, ignites your own Jupiter-Pluto square ready to judge your search for meaning. The following year a solar eclipse opposing your Jupiter and squaring your Pluto, issues the verdict. Be prepared for a wagging finger if your ethics are not up to par.

1999

In this last year of the '90s attention focused on two mysteries — the strange eclipses described by Nostradamus as threatening violence; and what became known as the Y2K problem. According to the ancient seer, the anti-Christ would appear with the four horsemen of the apocalypse, or something like that! Y2K was about the adaptability of technology, whether the computer systems which organized society would continue to work when dates changed from 1999 to 2000. Astrologers were more concerned with the fixed grand cross which does symbolize those horsemen and their belligerent stubbornness. The interactions of Mars opposing Saturn, the solar eclipse opposing Uranus, and Jupiter opposing Neptune, made this a year of tension when a whole set of new "rages" were named — road rage, air rage, office rage, phone rage etc. Yes, it was an angry time.

The first warning for the souls arriving now will be to avoid destructive confrontations and learn to use the practicality of Taurus, with the generosity of Leo and Scorpio's capacity for sharing so that the communal freedom of

Aquarius can be established. The alternative is potential frustration and force that cause world wars.

Having Uranus and Neptune in Aquarius indicate that spiritual change is required to welcome a New Age. This should be obvious to you. For most of this century awareness of outside forces has been coming gradually. With the interest in crop circles, UFOs and angels, humanity is admitting it does not know everything. Since the Aquarian eclipse, in 1962, evidence of the need for higher principles has been growing. Many military coups released waves of protests against old controls. Then the passage of Pluto through Scorpio from 1984 brought buried corruption to the surface. Seeing the dark side helps to avoid repeating history and you have a special key to open minds — Chiron.

The year ends on a dramatic note when Chiron conjoins Pluto in Sagittarius, for the first time since 1941, which was the low-point of the second world war. Then they met in Leo and the two ends of Chiron's bridge, Saturn and Uranus, were in Taurus, suggesting that materialism was dominating the ego. In Sagittarius the Chiron-Pluto healing can be philosophical as well as spiritual, adding wisdom to the search for perfection. The points of tension this time are from Aquarius to Taurus as Uranus and Saturn make a waxing square. Material limitations could challenge the urge for freedom.

Jupiter zips through three signs this year, so it is not wise to rely on Lady Luck, or expect the law, to be logical. That could make gamblers nervous if they are relying on a big win to solve all problems. Blaming, striking or suing someone else may not be the answer to wealth, either. The enlightened souls now being born will be able to respect the material world wisely, and be ready to "live on the Earth lightly".

This is not a year to be gloomy, but time to be realistic and responsible, and that is a good way to grow up. The notorious fixed cross of August gives options to deal with its tensions. Actions can be motivated by responsibility, courage and strong-mindedness or Me first, anger, frustration, and rebellion. As the Nodes call for a balance between Leo and Aquarius that could mean stepping into a new age with big-heartedness, like "let's have a party, and you are all invited."

GENERATIONS

The measure of a generation may be any length. As defined by the Oxford dictionary it includes all the people born at a particular time and/or in a certain stage of development. For astrological purposes such a grouping can be measured by the transits of the slowest planets, Pluto, Neptune and Uranus. As they move through the signs they provide a common theme for everyone born into that time.

The energies of these transpersonal planets can be applied in many different ways, beneficially or destructively. Sometime in the '70s a phrase often heard was "sex, drugs and rock and roll", which certainly describes some uses of those three planets. Other interpretations could be power, faith and intelligence, or violence, escapism and revolt. In reverse order they symbolize the "Light, Love and Power to restore the plan on Earth" of the Great Invocation, a mantra much used in the new age.

The patterns made by these outer planets are imprinted somewhere in our destiny, and, depending on how we respond to their tests, will be viewed as either an emotional crisis requiring difficult decisions; a phase of history to be endured; or as a particular strength to share with others. The signs they are in express how each planet will be experienced, and the houses of your chart will show the area of life that will be most affected. Even though we share their position in the zodiac with people born in a span of many years it does matter how we use them as individuals.

Noticing the synchronicity of their cycles explains many subtle undercurrents that form a background to our personal lives. Aside from their effects on our own charts, it is possible to look at history as a panoramic backdrop for each generation, then plot the waves of change in this century.

History is always seen from a subjective point-of-view, as are the descriptions here of the 20th century. You may translate events and trends in your own way and come to different conclusions. But, however we interpret experiences, taking a broad view of what has happened, and is happening, can give some shape to the immense changes that have taken place within living memory. As the patterns of slow planets change and different combinations occur, humanity has a choice between trying to ignore them or doing something to manifest their planetary energies positively.

Any cycle begins with a conjunction and unfolds into its hard aspects of waxing square, opposition, and waning square, before it starts the next one. The years of these hard aspects link in some way to the year of the conjunction which was the seeding point for new growth. We were all born into different stages of specific ongoing lessons and have a part to play in their outcome.

Those born in the years of major conjunctions such as 1947, 1952, 1965, 1982, 1989 and 1993 have a special aptitude for dealing with their messages, but we all have to learn how to handle them sometime. Having to work personally with these universal energies, which were unknown 200 years ago, is a relatively modern phenomenon. This makes the 20th century a special time in human evolution and an exciting time to be alive.

The Big Picture

With the variable speed of planets the spans of generations overlap, but by shaping them approximately to Pluto's slow pace there have been five main groups completed since WWI, with the sixth beginning in 1996. Each one has had its difficulties and challenges, its strengths and weaknesses, bringing new components to a rapidly developing global family.

The first stretched from war to war with its anxieties, escapism and depression:
- Pluto in Cancer from 1914 to 1939
- Neptune in Leo from 1915 to 1929, then in Virgo until 1942
- Uranus in Aries from 1927 to 1934, and Taurus until 1942

Roaring '20s

The second took us from war into rock and roll, increase in armaments and national suspicions, to the birth of computer geniuses and the Boomers. This was the bridge from the clashes of dictators to wider global communication, opening minds to new ways of viewing the world:
- Pluto in Leo from 1939 to 1957
- Neptune into Libra in 1942 to 1956
- Uranus in Gemini from 1942 to 1948 then in Cancer until 1956

Depressing '30s

Fighting '40s

The third, starting with Sputnik, turned attention to space and new freedoms, bringing excess and addictions with its inflated egos and shock at the loss of heroes. Expectations of a better future were raised then dashed, disturbing the sense of continuity:
- Pluto was in Virgo from 1957 to 1971
- Neptune in Scorpio from 1956 to 1970
- Uranus in Leo from 1956 to 1962, then Virgo until 1968 and Libra until 1974

Frantic '50s

Protesting '60s

The fourth was a time of fallen idols and a shaking up of ignorance. Political and economic disappointments dispelled old dreams of stability and strange patterns in gender relationships were emerging:
- Pluto was in Libra from 1971 to 1984
- Neptune was in Sagittarius from 1970 to 1984
- Uranus in Scorpio from 1974 to 1982

Disillusioning '70s

The fifth group has delved even deeper into the unknown, uncovering old knowledge, exposing embarrassing secrets and spreading information. With the revelations came a loss of faith in once-respected institutions that will have to be regained sooner or later, but good reputations take time to build and are quickly destroyed. Self-preservation seemed important as crime, greed and disease brought a growing defensiveness but it also had the effect of refocusing responsibility closer to home:
- Pluto in Scorpio from 1984 to 1996
- Neptune in Capricorn from 1984 to 1998
- Uranus in Sagittarius from 1982 to 1989 then Capricorn until 1996.

Excessive '80s

Exposing '90s

As the next group appears, with its concentration on fire and air whipping up religious and philosophic fervor, the world is facing an uncertain future with new ideas and enthusiasms as well as a good dose of optimism to "carry on regardless":
- Pluto is in Sagittarius from 1996 to 2008
- Neptune in Aquarius from 1998 to 2011
- Uranus in Aquarius from 1996 to 2003, then into Pisces until 2011 completing its cycle from 1927.

Perhaps the most urgent lesson at this time comes from Pluto.

Pluto

The most recent planet to be identified, Pluto is something of a mystery in its size and orbital behavior. There is still much to learn about its symbolism. It was first seen in 1930, when Uranus (change) was in Aries ready for something new, and Neptune (faith) in Virgo to be re-analyzed and made productive. Pluto itself was in Cancer. Although it had not been seen before then, it was already known to exist since 1912. An interesting coincidence is that at the earlier date Pluto was at exactly the same degree of Gemini as Uranus had been when it was discovered, and Uranus was in its own sign of Aquarius. A cosmic hint of the approach of a new age.

At present Pluto represents the dark side of Self which is neither good nor bad in itself but if left unattended can grow moldy like a piece of cheese left too long in the basement. Not an energy to be ignored forever. As human beings work at becoming more conscious of their own complexity, it is important to acknowledge that we all have a shadow that is at odds with the nice person we try to be. By admitting its existence, at least to ourselves, the energy wasted in keeping it hidden is released. In this final decade of the century the unpleasant smell of neglected mistakes is choking us. It is time to clean up.

Since Pluto was first seen, there have been six different generations born as the planet moved from Cancer to Sagittarius, where it will remain until 2008. With its irregular orbit Pluto's length of stay in each sign varies, averaging about 13½ years, in its cycle of approximately 250 years. For about 20 years of each cycle its influence is at its strongest when it moves inside the orbit of Neptune as it did in 1979. Then, because it is closest to the Sun it moves at its fastest speed. This happens when it is in its own sign of Scorpio, time for a "descent into hell". Plumbing the depths of human nature it forces into light whatever has been hidden, and destroys whatever is decaying. Then it fertilizes new seeds from the results.

This process can be uncomfortable. Past exploitation, or corruption are revealed as warnings that we do not really get away with anything. We just think we do. Like the karmic boomerang effect associated with Saturn, Pluto brings back the garbage and dumps it for all to see as a reminder that it has to be dealt with.

Pluto shows up in many guises. In the final chapter of the 20th century evidence of violence, pollution and pornography, which are really the same thing, are coming at us from all directions. Poisoning of natural resources, adulterated food, misleading advertising, violent TV, economic manipulation, rising crime, dishonest authorities, child and spouse abuse, and on and on. Seeing the negative effects of such exploitation wakes us up to the dangers of misused power and how it contaminates our lives.

In any chart Pluto represents a painful lesson to be learned about power and how it is being used by us, or by those we allow to exercise it over us. Do we really like being manipulated by hidden forces, whatever they are? And who benefits? It does not help to get paranoid, but it is wise to admit we have often been fooled, ignorant or even apathetic about what goes on in this shrinking world. That is not a wise way to travel through this chaotic era. There are too many dragons waiting to devour the unwary.

This little cosmic body spells drama. Operas, tragedies and myths about jealousy and death describe its symptoms in strong terms which seem to have little to do with normal life. But in this century these destructive undercurrents in our nature are demanding a new look.

Everyone has Pluto somewhere in their chart pointing out an area where our darker motives have to be faced. That is not an easy project for anyone and it is a task we have to deal with as an individual, separate from the mass. Otherwise we are in danger of being swept up in the hysteria of a mob behaving in a way that we would not do alone. An orator's ability to sway a crowd; the blood-lust of a lynch mob; the fanaticism of some religious groups, can all lead to waves of emotion condoning actions that would shame the individuals involved once they pull free.

Being the god of the underworld, Pluto works to bring hidden flaws to the surface so that conscious decisions can be made about the use and abuse of power. In legends he is a frightening figure, with his face invisible beneath his helmet, and round his waist is a belt hung with many skulls. Not the kind of fellow one wants to meet. We try hard to avoid dealing with this weird character but Pluto as a friend is the source of riches. He is not corrupt but his role is to check our willingness to stand up to corruption and refuse opportunities that are tempting but dishonest. The heads on Pluto's belt are trophies, marking the number of times the ego has been defeated in the process of proving our worth. Facing the dark side takes the courage of a Luke Skywalker confronting Darth Vader.

As the 20th century has unrolled, more and more skeletons have fallen out of individual closets showing how the corruption of a vital energy has turned destructive. Power, in varying degrees, is something we all have, usually without realizing it.

Pluto's urge to transmute requires the releasing of negative tendencies so that more constructive ones can take their place. This is the symbolism of atom-splitting, which, in itself is not good or bad but the manner in which it is applied is vital to the outcome. Pluto offers black-and-white choices and its approximately 250-year cycle is concerned with illustrating the collective attitude towards slavery in all its forms and transforming it to a more civilized state.

When the planet has been explored more thoroughly its exact meaning may become clearer. In the meantime it can be summed up as the tempter, dangling opportunities with concealed motives. And we have to make the choices. The decisions we take show the intensity of feeling operating in that particular circumstance. Becoming conscious of our involvement in the whole places a new moral burden on us all as individuals. But each generation has a different kind of dragon to slay.

1914-1939 in Cancer

For our grandparents and great-grandparents the lesson of Pluto's influence was not apparent until it was seen, even though by 1912 it was known to exist. From 1914 in the sign of Cancer, it associated security with control and produced intense emotional need to possess, keeping too tight a grip on family, bank account or country. The lesson to be learned with Pluto in this sign is to let go and share emotional nurturing and the resources that sustain life. Historically, that "war to end all wars" began by testing obsessions of loyalty, with young men marching cheerfully behind a flag in the old traditional manner of sacrificing gladly for "king and country". But by the desperate year of 1917, destruction was too obvious for the call of duty to be easy. The carnage of a modern war was a shock that would show the high price of national glory and question the wisdom of holding on to possessions such as colonies, natural resources, even family members.

Cancer wants security but when, in the Treaty of Versailles in 1919, the dark side of wealthier nations imposed reparations on destitute ones, the result was wide-spread starvation leading to Depression and another war when Pluto changed signs in 1939.

The '30s illustrated how destructive extremism and dependency can be. When the schism widened between far-right and far-left, dictators herded demoralized masses who had lost the means of self-support.

Such insights can be clear to those born in the '30s with patterns of international tension imprinted on their psyches. How dependent the dispossessed become when individual ability to live life for themselves is taken away. Pluto warns against trying to possess. The dark side of Cancer can be emotionally smothering if it demands too much dependency. This applies to nations as well as families and with Pluto's control in a needy sign many possessive mothers held sway during these 25 years.

Pluto in Cancer is personified by the rich banker who refuses to loan instead of helping others develop their own talents. Starting with worldwide depression and famine, in the 1920s and "dirty thirties", reaction to the misused power of the wealthy took hold with a corresponding strengthening of dictatorships. When security in money and jobs was lost desperation took its place and tensions between the powerless and the powerful brought a rise in fascism and interest in communism to restore a balance. As unemployment grew people seeking work migrated and banded together forming mass movements (Pluto). This produced strikes and demonstrations on one hand and harsh methods of control on the other. What followed was the gathering of power into few hands with the excuse of defending security. This often brought mass round-ups and possible elimination of those causing political unrest. A reaction that is still in vogue in many countries. The lesson here was that too much manipulation, on either side, could be deadly.

People in the forefront of Cancer's need to share were born in 1931-32, when the level of insecurity was high. The karmic planet, Saturn, in the karmic sign of Capricorn, was opposing Pluto, which adds up to some heavy-duty responsibilities mixed with power struggles. Having the planets of control facing each other from difficult signs, suggests that you, more than others, should try to encourage cooperation in matters of authority, perhaps when you are a parent or a public official. The see-saw effect of this opposition can bring problems from someone depending too heavily on you, or you on them. Smothering parents need to ease up on emotional control.

One way to break any cycle of insecurity would be to share responsibility and material possessions. Have a good yard sale!

1939-1957 in Leo

The beginning and end of the period between 1939 and 1957, while Pluto worked its way through Leo, was of the chalk to cheese variety. Anyone who lived through this time as an adult knows the difference from start to finish of that 28 years. It was a time when national loyalties were coming to the crunch and idealism and social values were about to undergo critical reassessment. But there was still a great reluctance to face reality in 1939. Although it was the beginning of an ending, the tearing away from innocence took a long time.

Looking back it is hard not to blush when admitting how ignorant most of us were, just naive babes politically-speaking, sliding into a war that took away any pretensions of privilege that the "dirty thirties" had left behind. War was a leveler when bombs brought those at home into as much danger as those on the "front line".

Individuals born in this period, and there were a lot of post-war babies, have a great deal to offer the world. Pluto, the ultimate urge to control, needs your personal understanding of the delicacy with which positions of dominance should be handled. Pluto in Leo is the combination that tests the oft-used phrase, "power corrupts and absolute power corrupts absolutely." Your use of power and the leadership that goes with it will determine whether we come through the critical end-of-century years and start the 2000s with joy or horror.

From 1939 onwards, the world stage was set for a knock-down-drag-'em-out power play with ego drives at full throttle. Like a chess game, countries took up positions of advantage or self-protection. Germany invaded Czechoslovakia. Italy invaded Albania. Germany invaded Poland, forcing all of Europe into World War11. Then the USSR invaded Finland. The war brought out the stubbornness of the dictators, then when they had exhausted the world, by 1945, the wave of post-war babies known as the Boomers arrived on the scene, to show that power should have, or could have, a different use. This was the beginning of an end to out-dated ideas about security, but not quite the end itself as the stubbornness of fixed signs assures that nobody would give way easily.

People born into this background, specially around 1946-48 when Saturn was conjunct Pluto ready to restructure power, are challenged to control the urge to be bossy and to use their determination without causing log-jams. The generation of great egos was just beginning and even if you were not there when they were handed out, more than the usual number of you would like to be president of something. If you have self-doubts it is possible that you cover them well.

A major ego test probably started for you in 1984-85 when Pluto squared your Pluto as it did for everyone born in the first few years of the '40s. This occurred during, or soon after, your mid-life shake-up from Uranus, making the decade of the '80s a point of great personal transformation. Looking back at that time could show how well you survived Pluto's demands.

When the Boomers began to take center stage in the '90s old foundations were crumbling. The way these new arrivals choose to rebuild their societies will show how this wave of humanity has dealt with their own Pluto-egos.

Among the questions awaiting humanity back then was one of material values. And those of you born into this period, specially the second half of it, are likely to have been challenged by them, if you wanted stability and expected a settled life with a nice pension. Somewhere along the way it could have dawned on you that was an empty aim. Equating your bank account with your own worth may leave you confused. If you still have some fear of losing what you feel belongs to you — possessions or income, or whatever you use to measure your importance — think again. The choice is not between installing an alarm system, and training a pair of Doberman pinchers to patrol your estate or throwing everything away and living with a begging bowl. That loaded word "sacrifice" can just be part of a balance that makes life more enjoyable if you find it. You were born into a time of radical change when the goals were too distant to be recognizable. There was a long period when we all seemed to be floundering through change for change's sake but the reasons are clearer by now.

1957-1971 in Virgo

As Pluto slipped into Virgo the emotional emphasis moved from Self to service. These years would explain the need for discrimination in many areas which were of equal importance to rich and poor. It was the start of a process of separating those who want to control from those who want to serve.

The power of work and workers would begin to show, with unions gaining strength. But those associated with the Mafia had to be cleaned up. And they were. Then some demanded too much, so the pendulum swung back to anti-union feeling by the '80s when interest rates shot up and the job squeeze started. Pluto always offers the opportunity to go too far before seeing the results.

Another Virgo focus is on public health. As new building materials began polluting the work environment, bosses and employees were equally affected. You will be the generation which experiences the abolition of smoking in the work place and eventually has to take all pollution seriously. Recycling as a necessity will come in your lifetime, too.

People born in this period can uncover new knowledge and new interest in such subjects as preventative medicine and herbal remedies. When powerful medical communities, fearing competition, challenge their use, doctors with entrenched egos will be exposed. Official health plans need to be more open-minded for everyone's sake.

This was a wild time of mind-expanding drugs and psychedelic fashion as well as serious resistance to law-makers. Some of you pushed life to the limits and too many committed suicide in their teens, while others chose to work with dedication. The war in Vietnam was destroying old loyalties when your parents asked a good question, "why was it being fought at all?" Many of them burned their draft-cards and joined thousands in protest marches. This was only the beginning of a rising clamor for answers about who made the rules and who had to serve.

A cycle of approximately 120 years was completed during your early years with the Uranus and Pluto conjunction in 1965-6. This dramatic duo offered the choice of destructive rebellion or concern for individual freedom, with Virgo leaning towards helping others to find it. Past history was being tidied up and the barriers of class-consciousness were being broken down. In a few short years the public scene changed from the elegance of Camelot to the wildness of Woodstock. Virgo has a right to criticize and after the first wave of the Pluto in Leo generation matured and questioned authority at every level, a useful role for Pluto in Virgo was applying common sense to the use of power in any circumstance.

1971-1984 in Libra

In Libra, Pluto's task was to test out relationships. The healthy ones survived, but many with cracks in their structure broke down and divorce rates rose. People born between these years would have to face the need to cooperate and negotiate in new ways if they want a harmonious life.

Libra can be an influence for peace or extremism, with either the skill to mediate or the fighting spirit of its opposite sign, Aries. Pluto's aim here was to promote justice and, in case proof was needed, evidence of injustice has been pouring out ever since.

The early years of this generation saw the peak of terrorism and hijacking when the dispossessed started acting out their frustrations.

As children of the Boomers you are a generation living with the results of their excesses and can choose to continue them or go the opposite way. Many of the Boomers were idealistic in a world that had not yet discovered its limits, but you are dealing with a shrinking society where altruism will be needed to solve problems. When you mature your choice will be to continue the violence, as many of you have done in your own streets, or bring new justice to your society, negotiating with the extremes and proving that "we are all in this together".

Until governments get the message that we all have a right to be here, violence will continue between countries and within countries, with the added danger of it getting more sophisticated. The roots of injustice, or assumed injustice, are going to have to be rooted out.

Many governmental actions in this period were divisive and had disastrous international repercussions. Lobbyists were giving financial support to "tame leaders" who turned out to be greedy dictators or drug czars. Your generation will have to weigh the evidence of many decisions taken then and reconsider them. Choosing sides between Iran/Iraq, China/Taiwan, the two Koreas, or in civil wars, usually depended on interference by unseen forces tipping the scale. A lesson to learn from the results of such meddling was that manipulation on one side upsets the natural balance which groups might have found for themselves if left alone. A positive Libra approach would be to negotiate unity with the help of a powerful mediator, as in the Camp David Accords, for example. Someone has to find a balance, and that may be you.

The Star Wars trilogy, started in 1977, caught public imagination with its symbolism of the Plutonian fight between right and wrong and the need to respect an instinctive spiritual energy, the power of the Force.

1984-1996 in Scorpio

Pluto as a cleansing process is at its ultimate strength in Scorpio and washed plenty of "dirty linen" in public view in this period. Having shifted inside the orbit of Neptune it was now unusually close to Earth, ready to bring more piles of garbage to the surface.

Many of the skeletons due to tumble out of closets had been locked away for years. But when shock after shock hit the headlines with facts about political, economic and social corruption the public's faith in its chosen representatives was badly damaged and killed respect for many institutions.

Looking back at this period it is possible to see the extent of decay at the roots of many organizations which was being ignored until it was nearly too late. The proverbial "stitch in time" was not being made, and problems which should have been fixed early got out of hand. With Scorpio intensity, revelations of secret deals and questionable antics among reputable establishments were bad enough to give us a good dose of paranoia for years to come. But at least they were being revealed.

From 1986 Uranus was forming a warning aspect to Pluto (a semi-square) in their cycle begun in 1965. Other hints were coming from occult directions, like the appearance of the Blue Star predicted by the Hopi, and the Harmonic Convergence, concluding that a long, long era was coming to an end. Then came signs of hidden disturbances at home, with a rash of teen-age suicides, homeless people sleeping on the streets, a sudden plunge of the stock market, and in Washington, pieces of the ceilings over the statues of Thomas Jefferson and Abraham Lincoln began to fall! It was not "business as usual" in the US.

Scorpio is associated with insurance and in the '90s many kinds of disasters have strained financial protection to the limit, with enormous amounts needed to cover damages from floods, fires, tornadoes, and earthquakes. Nature was fighting back with its change of weather patterns all over the world. As emotional intensity increased so have cancer, and AIDS and there may be some connection. At the same time many new cures have been found. In your lifetime, medical needs could be revolutionized and, as the human spirit evolves, birth and death could be accepted as just different stages of life's spiral.

1996-2008 in Sagittarius

This time will be a lesson in compulsiveness and obsession, revealing a startling increase in the hidden worlds of addiction and abusive sexuality. The dark side of human nature is being exposed as rape, incest, and other kinky habits, are brought into public view, sometimes long after the event. Sagittarius, the teacher, is spreading the news abroad rather than restricting it to the neighborhood, so it has to be faced with shame. There is no great comfort in knowing that foreign gossip will be just as unpleasant as the home-grown variety, but the very quantity of deviation from what has been considered the norm, will demand reaction.

By the end of the century, another of Pluto's exposes could be about how wealth on a large scale is being procured and spent. The anguish of Depression after WWI, led to dictatorships, and was a reminder of the negative effect of shortages. A repeat of that lesson in the late '40s after the destruction of WWII, was met with the generosity of the Marshall Plan, a far-seeing effort to rebuild Europe. But again, in the 1990s, the extremes of haves and have-nots on all continents brought another world crisis.

Resources need to be shared not hoarded but a negative Pluto dams up wealth by holding on in fear of losing personal security instead of allowing money to flow. We are told that there is enough food and money to provide adequately for everyone on this planet if they are well distributed and not hidden under someone's mattress.

When money laundering and multinational dirty dealings are unmasked the lines of economic control can be mapped. Then at least we would know why governments cannot cope with deficits. But what do we do about it? Ah, that is our choice, not Pluto's.

Exchange of positive knowledge is due too, as ancient beliefs are exhumed for modern consideration. The benefit of having this intense energy in the optimistic sign could be that once the message has been received, the clean-up will be taken seriously and acted upon fast. Too many doomsayers offer little hope that decay can be stopped. But Pluto, the healer par excellence, has the whole world in his surgery and may be ready for some radical operations.

Neptune

In 1846, Neptune, planet of the universal spirit and higher level of Venus, was first seen. It was in Aquarius, conjunct Saturn, the old ruler of that sign, with Uranus in Aries, ready to take new action. Neptune introduced a longing for a more perfect world and a very difficult lesson about martyrdom and missions. It was time to dissolve the old rules and have faith in universal love where everyone could worship independently and "love one another" in their own way.

Attempting to "save the world" and telling the "natives" what to believe and how to behave was really doing Saturn's work of paternalism. When Neptune came into the picture Karl Marx was introducing his new religion and though it is difficult to associate the communism adopted by Russia as love the original aim of Marxism was certainly to shape a more perfect world. Perfection, like beauty, is in the eye of the beholder and can be very egotistical. At that time, the authority of Saturn squashed the compassion of Neptune, once again telling the natives what to do. The results have been disastrous, spawning suspicion between governments and, eventually, of governments.

The meaning of this planet that rules the Piscean Age, which Earth has been experiencing for the last two thousand years, has been surrounded by both confusion and deception. But now the age is ending it is time to clear up the misinterpretations and begin to enjoy its gifts.

This planet of sensitivity and creativity is not as gentle as it sounds. The god of the sea can initiate a fierce undertow if we do not get his message to go with the flow. When we get lost in stale dreams Neptune is like the tide rolling in to demolish our sand castles so we have to build new ones. Anything that has completed its usefulness is swept away, leaving a clean surface for a new start.

Its positive application is the simple Christ message of unconditional love, which has been so garbled over the centuries. And that means having compassion even when we do not like each other. It is also an urge to creativity through the wonder of natural beauty with all five senses. In its negative form, the Neptunian urge can become deceit and fantasy or escape into dreamland which, if carried too far, becomes a cop out from taking responsibility for one's own behavior. The addictions of today come from the search for pleasure in the wrong places, like drugs or alcohol.

In any chart Neptune can bring an experience of disappointment, drowning old assumptions concerning the sign it is in. It is the reminder to remove the rose-colored glasses and be realistic about expectations.

Earlier this century, the Ageless Wisdom of Alice A. Bailey talked of immense changes that would take place in human understanding particularly about the meaning of love (Neptune). Bailey taught that seven rays are enlightening planet Earth and guiding humans towards a higher level of evolution. She described the ray of devotion and idealism, (Ray 6) with its crusading fanaticism as slowly fading while the ray of love/wisdom and mystical vision (Ray 2) was taking over. This means that the era of active crusading is ending. Concern for others remains but needs more thought and less aggression. Jehads and religious zealots are out of date.

Getting a grasp on Neptune is not easy. Perhaps it is time to acknowledge that there is something new to be learned about the meaning of love. With its 14-year stay in each sign, there have been eleven generations since its discovery. The twelfth starts in 1998, when it enters Aquarius again.

1915-1929 in Leo

The First World War was launched while Neptune was at the end of the sign of Cancer, bringing the shocks that would expose illusions about security. Watching a few episodes of Upstairs, Downstairs, it is easy to see how much adjusting was going to be done in a very short time. That war was the tide to end an era of privilege then start another that would undermine the pride of empires.

The decade of the '20s was unrealistic in trying to cling to past glory. Hollywood took over dreams and, for many, has not let go since. Those born in this period had parents who knew the highs and lows of confidence when their good times were swept away in two world wars, then reality had to be faced. Children born with Neptune in Leo experienced their own war and the dissolution which followed. It has not been easy to understand your children either whose dreams were fashioned in the '60s when good times were, once again, yanked away in a chaos of assassinations and protests. If your sense of self was not drowned in the constant tides of expectation and let-down, you may have salvaged your own brand of faith and be more inclined to go with its flow.

When Neptune was first seen it was at the same degree as the US Moon, at 26 Aquarius, promising a period of emotional confusion and that led to a civil war which devastated a nation. It reached the opposition to that degree in 1927 when its Leo dreams were due to be shattered by the 1929 crash, just as it moved into Virgo. It will return to 26 Aquarius in 2010.

1929-42 in Virgo

Neptune in Virgo can be an uncomfortable mix of serving and suffering. While sorting through the aftermath of the economic crash and approach of another war, your parents lived through confusing years, probably affecting your sense of security. Pluto's cycle with Neptune which started in 1891, reached a semi-square in 1930-32, warning of growing tensions. When drought and unemployment threatened people's ability to nourish themselves it was time to notice hidden faults in the working world (Virgo), before they got worse. And they did.

Unhealthy values within the financial system denied many people the means to support their families while others gained too much. In a climate of desperation, strikes and protest marches brought people together to form unions. Echoes of Karl Marx! But a wise American president introduced welfare.

Many of you born into this anxious time have been very sensitive to the needs of the disadvantaged. Humanitarians ready to work in a serving profession have had plenty to accomplish in your lifetime. Too young to fight in WWII you were the right age to be involved in peace corps and international aid projects. Provided you used some Virgo discrimination when handing out welfare and charity rather than being dewy-eyed idealists or bleeding-hearts, you have followed your purpose and could feel fulfilled.

As you matured, through the exciting '60s and into the '70s you may have been well aware that a familiar world was coming to an end. If your practical antennae were tuned to society's trends your anxiety quotient may have risen faster than for those less sensitized. The job market was uncertain for your parents and, in the '90s, when you were ready to retire it was unsettled again, leaving some of you, or your children, faced with a foggy future. Neptune's Virgo message to "keep the faith, baby" was your cry in the '70s when you were concluding that the Universe might meet your practical needs, but not necessarily your wants.

1942-56 in Libra

These were the years of the baby boom, a mass influx that would change society. The experiences of such a sensitive planet in the sign of partnerships produced a potential for both sadness and delight. Neptune dissolves whatever has lost its usefulness, and in Libra the focus was on the traditional ways of cooperating. Chances are that many of you from this generation had something painful to learn about relating, especially if you were expecting too much. Disappointments taught you that a happy-ever-after ending is only a myth if it anticipates a perfection beyond human capacity.

If you were born in 1952-53 when Saturn conjoined Neptune, many of you experienced broken homes with parents who had lost their dreams. The disillusions of the post-war world encouraged escapism and many adults were drinking their way to oblivion. In 1954-55 Uranus reached its waning square to Neptune, forcing reality for your lesson in dealing with families and partners. That was a difficult undertaking if it left you feeling lonely and misunderstood by those closest to you. But any tendency you had towards escapism needed to be tidied up before the next conjunction of Uranus and Neptune, in 1993.

A lot was happening in the saga of communism, a political dream that had turned into a nightmare. This was the height of McCarthyism in the US with near hysteria of finding a "red under every bed" leading to suspicion and blacklisting falling on suspected left-wing sympathizers. But in the country of its origin, the USSR, Stalin had just died and a deadly struggle for more enlightened leadership was underway. It would take a long time for a winner to emerge. But the tide had turned.

On a happier note, Neptune in Libra is a search for harmony and a sense beauty. With Saturn it can bring out your artistic side providing a frame for your own dreams and challenging you to tone down your expectations of relationships. From 1950 until the end of the century, Neptune formed an aspect of opportunity (sextile) to Pluto, which blends two important urges — to have faith (Neptune) and to destroy in order to renew (Pluto). Libra's influence is to weather the storm as calmly as you can. Its dream is to find peace in your time.

1956-1970 in Scorpio

Neptune in Scorpio was a dangerous time for addictions and intense unreality. This combination at its worst symbolizes the intensity of escapism that can lure the unwary into the destructive world of alcohol, drugs or sex. Not to mention jealousy or obsession. All the illusions that Scorpio can trap and test. The search for Nirvana that Neptune was undertaking led along dangerous paths with seductive music and LSD. Many young people who would become your parents were seeking transcendental experiences or flocking to India on spiritual pilgrimages.

The planet of love descended into hell increasing fascination with orgies and overdoses. In 1964 the Pill was available, taking away the fear of pregnancy and the following year, the Summer of Love in San Francisco lasted 15 months with its escapism into sexual bliss and crazy love-ins. On the outside, attention turned to space with its dreams of finding Shangri-la somewhere far away from the pollution of Earth. UFO stories increased.

It was also a time when idealists were ready to use talents for the benefit of the less fortunate, and practice the message of Neptune in Virgo. The bare-foot doctors of China; the Peace Corps and store-front lawyers in the US were groups helping to conquer the ego and seed new dreams, asking "Not what your country can do for you but what you can do for your country".

Hidden psychic powers were being renewed, with the appearance of new forms of healing and the revival of witchcraft in modern guise. Your group is ready to accept alternative medicine and healing through herbs, or color and sound.

This period was the start of a dissolution of traditional power, even though the full effect would not show until your generation came into its own, 30 years later.

Scorpio provides a background of confrontation presenting opportunities to face the "enemy" and eliminate old mistakes, then prepare for a rebirth by sowing new, healthier seeds for the future.

The splitting of the atom illustrates the kinds of life and death options facing the world. The power released can be fission, a pulling apart, or fusion, a melding together. Either extreme can be deadly unless it is used constructively. The choices we make both as individuals and as part of a collective show how much is understood about our need to evolve. Emotional, mental and environmental garbage has been building up for centuries and it is time for a "trash bash" with your generation leading the way.

1970-84 in Sagittarius

The philosophy of Sagittarius brought new kinds of worship when Neptune arrived there in 1970. This was a time when the Boomers left home and took you with them. Young people were exploring the world with backpacks and goodwill. If they found their gurus, it is likely that you were introduced to many cultures and religions in your life. Universal dreams were being exchanged around the globe in an atmosphere of hope.

This generation can make some international dreams possible if it accepts reality and stays optimistic. But first the expansiveness of Sagittarius would bring waves of wishful thinking and drugs for escapism. Multinational organizations began to gobble each other up, only to lose out to bigger, greedier ones. The international drug trade grew fast at this time and with little hope of being controlled until the late '90s, at the end of Neptune's stay in Capricorn.

With the symbol of oil (Neptune) in the sign of exploration (Sagittarius) this product was instrumental in inflating many economies and influencing foreign policies. From 1970 the price of oil was raised by Libya, then OPEC, and in 1975 the terrorist known as the Jackal staged a daring kidnapping at a meeting of oil chiefs in Vienna. Events such as the sudden rise and fall in prices, the installing of dictators friendly to oil companies and the Gulf war, have all been pulling the economic strings of the world with increasing persistence. A useful role for your imaginative generation could be to replace oil with a renewable source of some kind. By 1977 when the asteroid Chiron was discovered in Taurus, that was a hint that some healing was required in the way the natural resources of our planet were being treated.

A major change of focus came in 1979 as Pluto moved inside the orbit of Neptune, completing a cycle and sowing the seeds of the future. This was the year that began a demonstration of the dangers of power, with the election of Mrs. Thatcher, an explosion at the 3-Mile Island nuclear plant and the arrival of AIDS. Time for some serious contemplation of values and revision of dreams.

1984-98 in Capricorn

With the planet of confusion (Neptune) in the sign of authority (Capricorn), it is little wonder that governments everywhere came under suspicion. Political corruption and secret dealings were being uncovered by Pluto in Scorpio, surprising the public, even though such maneuvering had always existed. This period, more than any other in living memory, was responsible for unearthing skeletons of corruption for all to see.

When Neptune was photographed, in 1989, the picture down here on Earth was not so pretty. It was a year of oil spills and increasing use of drugs, with AIDS swamping the sexual form of love. Saturn was again conjunct Neptune, emphasizing the opportunity to restructure (Saturn) spirituality (Neptune) and to actualize in some material sense the beauty and infinite love that mystical Neptune encompasses.

People born into this period could form governments willing to serve unselfishly, which is a promise, or at least a possibility, of the 21st century.

When Uranus conjoined Neptune, in 1993-95 religious structures were changing. Traditional religions were losing ground to new kinds of spirituality. In this age of developed individuality most people have the freedom to worship in their own way. Some people claimed to be born-again or to be in touch with angels, while some joined fanatical cults perhaps founded in the Neptune in Scorpio period. No longer is it appropriate to go charging off to fight the good fight on someone else's behalf. We have to find our own salvation. It will be more effective to apply compassion to everyday matters and work to improve our own sphere.

Oil spills and natural disasters like tornadoes, earthquakes and floods have piled responsibility on government aid programs. Before Neptune left this sign the coffers were emptying, and expecting government to pay the bills may be increasingly wishful thinking.

Though we seemed to be living in depressing times as the reality of past mistakes become clearer by the end of the century, the possibilities of rebuilding (Capricorn) with faith and forgiveness (Neptune) was strong.

1998-2012 in Aquarius

This is where, in 1846, Neptune was first discovered in an exact conjunction with Saturn, and communism was born. The idealism of Neptune has caused many problems, and disappointments, since it became a conscious energy a 150 years ago while trying to get free from Saturn's trap of having to face facts. Each time these planets have met expectations have had to be lowered to meet reality. What has to be understood and accepted is that humans are dealing with both heaven (Neptune) and earth (Saturn) — spirit and material — at the same time.and need to find a balance between excess in either direction.

Neptune's next meeting with Saturn was in Taurus, in 1882, when industry was booming and floods of immigrants followed their dreams of wealth to North America. Next the planets met in Leo in 1917, when false dreams of heroic victory were shattered and confidence in leaders eroded. In Libra, around 1952, the burst bubbles of happy-ever-after brought different expectations to relationships. Their most recent conjunction, in Capricorn in that dramatic year of 1989 when walls, physical and ideological, were broken down, has questioned faith in governments, institutions and the old rules of hierarchy.

Now that Neptune is back in Aquarius, it could bring disappointments in reliance on technology. But a more enlightened version of common welfare or community caring could grow, and there should be some noticeable changes in social vision early in the new century. Keeping Neptune anchored to actuality is the key to its real benefits.

Perhaps we will not really perceive its message clearly until it comes full circle back to 26 degrees of Aquarius in 2009.

Uranus

The spirit of revolution was rising in 1781, when Uranus, in the sign of Gemini, was first discovered. The urge for independence, personal and collective, was about to emerge from the strictures of Saturn which until then had been the most distant of the seven planets visible in our solar system. When Saturn, the status quo, grows too rigid it needs to be moved out of the way and sometimes that takes immense effort. So Uranus had come along to shake things up with a few revolutions.

This new urge to rebel marked the beginning of the difficult task of using personal freedom with responsibility. Rebellion can be destructive so for the sake of law and order Uranus and Saturn have to find a balance between them. It has taken hundreds of years to learn and it still is not settled. These two contradictory urges have been battling it out ever since.

This planet of the universal mind, and higher octave of Mercury, was going to introduce the Information Age, with networks of international communication. In the last decade of the 20th century it is in its own sign, Aquarius, for the third time since it was discovered. (The other times were 1828 and 1912.) Now, with the Internet revolutionizing education and linking people of like-minds around the world there is little excuse to be ignorant.

Uranus is a planet containing a lot of unstable energy which can explode unexpectedly with little cause. The urge for radical change to make room for new growth will always be with us. Its purpose is to challenge and change ideas by blasting through the inertia. No wonder it has been called the Awakener.

Its 84-year cycle round the zodiac from Aries can be measured as a project with 12 chapters each one taking individuality to a higher lever of understanding, like a spiral. Moving into a new sign every seven years Uranus' upsets may seem like a seven-year-itch! As it moves through the signs, it signals a certain type of upheaval that will contribute to human evolution. People born into each generation can consider a particular kind of change as their personal contribution to mental development. Then each time it makes a square or opposition aspect to a natal position, it will bring personal change through disruptive or mind-opening ideas, if you are ready for them.

Every 30 years or so history offers hints, like report cards, on the state of change your generation is making. The circumstances may be different but the patterns are discernible if you look for them.

When Uranus conjoins either of the other two slow planets, Neptune or Pluto, it starts much longer lessons which overlap with this shorter cycle. Its slowest one, with Neptune, takes about 172 years and alters beliefs and ideals associated with sensitivity, compassion or worship. Their conjunction in 1819, in Sagittarius, concluded in 1993 when they met again in Capricorn. As that earlier circuit had begun before Neptune had arrived on the scene, Uranus was virtually working alone for one 84-year trip, until Neptune was discovered in 1846. By then Uranus in Aries had just begun another short cycle of initiative, of 84 years, which was completed by 1927.

When Neptune came into the picture, Uranus stirred up new meaning for the planet of divine love. For 172 years heads and hearts were learning to work together in the Sagittarian realms of philosophy, psychic ability and religion. Being born into the old cycle, which finished in 1993, has meant living through a time of confusion as knowledge increased and the world grew smaller. The final square of that long cycle came in the 1950s with a group of people who had new ideas to learn about nurturing each other and changing family values.

Uranus' conjunction with Pluto happens about every 115-127 years and is a more radical upheaval than its lesson with Neptune. A new one began recently, in the mid-1960s, when the revolutionary urge (Uranus) was ready to destroy (Pluto) old ideas and plant new ones that can bring a different political vision specially in the working world (Virgo). Since then Pluto has been throwing up political dirt like a spring-clean that was long overdue.

The previous cycle, started in 1850 at the 29th degree of Aries, made its waning square in the 1930s when the need for new vision could be seen clearly.

Learning to handle this volatile pair of energies is both dangerous and exciting but each new scene is set to give extra meaning to "We the people," as the masses take more and more control over their own lives.

The ripple effects of the most recent cycle, started in 1927 in Aries, can be traced through modern history as a work in progress. While making hard aspects when it moves through Cancer, Libra and Capricorn, Uranus has offered times for collective humanity to turn corners and either take action, (a waxing square); see clearly (an opposition); or face reality (a waning square). Until it starts the next cycle from Aries, in 2011, we are in a tidying up stage of an evolutionary phase, with 11 different generations already working to complete it. New thinking is accelerating the pace of our growing consciousness, shaking up the accepted ways of living, sometimes violently and sometimes more patiently, depending on the depths of frustration that has built up since the last cycle. People born at the time of the conjunction of 1965-66 are already pushing independence to its limit. In the process many of them have gone too far even though the time for definite action (waxing square) in this cycle will not come until 2011 when Pluto is in Capricorn and Uranus in Aries.

Again and again when Uranus arrives at the 29th degree of a sign events seem to add extra spice to its task, like a reminder to pay attention. It reaches the ends of Aquarius in 2003 and Pisces in 2010-11.

1927-34 in Aries

A cycle starting in the active sign of Aries in 1927 brought new initiatives in technology and the excitement of flying. But the primary lesson of the new Uranus cycle was about international aggression and the change of thinking needed to bring lasting peace to the world. The after-effects of destruction left by WWI could not be ignored and were warnings that war was an expensive way to settle differences

If you were born into the early part of this period, wars have continually intruded on your life. The need to rebel against old attitudes to aggression is imprinted on your psyche. Your childhood was upset by WWII and your youth by the Korean war, then if you lived in the US your children were ripe for Vietnam, or the turbulent time which followed it. Then your grandchildren were probably the right age for the Gulf war.

In 1932 Uranus was in a waning square to Pluto, in Cancer, and the "crisis of consciousness" this square brings was very evident in those agonizing years of post-war starvation. A world conference on disarmament took place and the League of Nations was formed to improve international relations. Unfortunately, the powers-that-be did not get the right message about keeping the peace. Using the military to secure power is quite different from using military power for security.

Within a few years the League fell apart and the world would have to wait for another world war to end, before a stronger international body, the United Nations, was established. The desperate plight of defeated countries encouraged future dictatorships which led your parents into WWII.

Proof of the anti-war bias of your Uranus cycle became clear when you were already mature. In 1965-66 when Uranus reached its conjunction with Pluto at 16 Virgo, tensions among people of military age were about to explode. The significance of that degree is that it was exactly square to the degree of the Pluto-Uranus opposition at 16 Gemini, in 1901, and was also the exact degree of Uranus at the end of WWII. This repeat of crises at similar degrees must say something to everyone born in the previous cycle, before 1927. You came to finish what was left incomplete by them.

Nature's drama of the 29 degrees of Aries brought two clear hints about the future. Dust storms stripping top soil in western states was a reminder to pay attention to our planet. In Europe Hitler became Fuehrer, the Nazi rallies and the Night of the Long Knives were preludes to another destructive period.

1934-42 in Taurus

The big changes for Uranus in Taurus are material ones. Banks were shaken up by panic and depression before the American president took control. Some changes were prompted by Franklin D. Roosevelt's welfare schemes and fireside chats but most were only temporary. In the '30s international financiers were still in charge and about to launch another profitable war. The price of gold was fixed, the dollar devalued in 1934, then came the Federal Reserve Act which set up a private body to control public funds, not necessarily for the public advantage. On and off the Feds' manipulation has been questionable. "Who is in control" will be the urgent question by the end of this century, when you are ready to retire.

By 1939 the world's stability was about to be shaken up and the Taurean responsibility for natural resources was pushed aside while the killing and destruction was renewed. This was the year the atom was split, with dramatic options for future existence. How that works out in future could be a heavy responsibility for you.

The shortages of war and losses from bombings changed priorities and attitudes to material possessions were turned upside down. But once again, that was only temporary. It would be another half century before our destruction of natural resources was taken seriously, when nature was hitting back with changed weather patterns. Major tests for your generation when you were ready to assume power, were altering the distribution of money and preserving the environment. Big undertakings which have not yet been tackled thoroughly.

You would have cause to distrust the war-mongers in the '60s when the draft for Vietnam was increased and finance was again being channeled into arms build-up. Then in the '90s the monetary squeeze was one of employment effecting your children's stability. Being the stewards of Mother Earth means having respect for her and removing any dams stopping the flow of nature's goodies. So that her gifts are distributed equably there is a need to keep giving and receiving in balance.

In 1941 the contrasting planets, Uranus and Saturn, were both at the last degree of Taurus bringing dangerous tension to humanity's roots. That was the year of a Lease-Lend agreement to supply the allies in Europe; then came the shock of Pearl Harbor. Additional messages of this conjunction are that natural materials would have to be preserved and that true wealth depended on protecting the power of planet Earth itself.

1942-48 in Gemini

Uranus in Gemini is an invitation to change trade and communications and in spite of, or because of, the war this was a beginning for new methods of universal exchange. Ironically the experiments of wartime brought many scientific leaps forward once the trading of modern technology started. Such discoveries as radar, rocketry and the micro-chip came into being at this time and they would eventually shrink the world to the size of a global village linked by computer. From now on traces of the "olden days" were fading as change followed change while you were growing up.

In the Ageless Wisdom, of Alice A. Bailey, the polarizing sign of Gemini is said to be where the soul is jogged to attention to prepare for a journey of initiation. Certainly the shocking years of the WWII were a wake-up call for humanity. When the bomb was dropped on Hiroshima, in 1945, the three slow planets had reached a crucial pattern. Pluto at the mid-point of Uranus and Neptune, presented a life-and-death choice that required deep thought and concern for our planet. The souls born at this time must take the choice seriously.

With the planet of the universal mind in Gemini plenty of mental energy poured into the world with your generation. You were in the forefront of social upset with the flower children, peaceniks and TV watchers. Destined to be computer whizzes and parents of exceptional children, you may experience competition between people and machines. If so, it is important to remember your humanness as a mental planet (Uranus) in a mental sign (Gemini) can get so cerebral it suppresses feelings.

If the symbolism of Uranus in Cancer means women's lib and Uranus in Leo men's lib, then your generation started kids lib. That makes it your responsibility to pay attention to the plight of youngsters. Before the end of the century many children had lost their bearings and needed help.

In the rush to productivity in the '40s everyone was needed and the role of individuals started to shift. At the time what was required was quantity, more planes, more guns and more ammunition. But when you were maturing international competition brought the need for new ideas. Far-seeing manufacturers began accepting workers' suggestions for better working methods, stimulating employee interest in the product.

This started a change of attitude to responsibility. Instead of being at the top or the bottom of a vertical system, where orders come down from above, people were having opportunities for more cooperation within a group. This new horizontal approach with its freedom to exchange ideas is one that your generation can encourage in your working life. In 1947 when the rebuilder (Saturn) met with the demolition of Pluto in Leo, your purpose of tearing down and renewing was all set.

The last gasp of Uranus in Gemini brought many changes in structure, like the blockade of Berlin, the partition of India, the birth of Israel and the Marshall plan to rebuild Europe. The '90s and the new century would bring opportunities for leadership in time to "build a bridge to the 21st century". Bridge building is an apt term for your purpose as spanning the gorge between thinking and feeling is the nature of your duality.

1948-56 in Cancer

Uranus in Cancer saw a shift in the expectations of emotional closeness. An interesting symbol was split-level homes. Much migrating and reestablishing of families broke up old ties. As a result of your restless traveling in the late '60s and '70s many of this generation looked for emotional closeness in groups or substituted friends for family. Some found an outlet for their emotions when they mobbed their new heroes, the Beatles and Rolling Stones.

There was little security in your childhood when parents and countries were trying to readjust after years of war. Emotional upsets have been common among your peers consequently your impression of home-life may be unusual. Problems arose when both males and females were unsure what to expect from each other and many had shaky marriages or felt unable to make emotional commitments. And as women took more authority in the work place a lot of social adjustment was needed.

The waxing square of Saturn to Uranus, in 1951, initiative to build emotional freedom, triggered women's lib and opened up new roles for you by the '70s and '80s. Certainly motherhood was going to be quite different by the time you had your babies. Yours is the generation which introduced alternatives to child-care with house-husbands taking over the kids while mother worked. In the '80s and '90s it has not been unusual for families to be made up of groups living together for convenience, necessity or desire, rather than just mum, dad and 1½ children.

Your children grew up in the chaotic years of the '80s and '90s when all values seem to be changing and schools had become war zones. If they find their own stability these kids can bring a new set of rules to their own parenting. A 21st century answer to Saturn's cooperation with Uranus could be tough love with a long rope and a delicate balancing act where closeness makes room for individual independence and caring accepts the need for freedom.

The shake up of the last degree of Cancer saw the Hungarian uprising, an effort which dispersed the people from a country which would not obtain its freedom until the late '80s when Uranus was about to move into the opposite sign, Capricorn.

1956-62 in Leo

The changes to be made by you were in leadership. With the ruler of Aquarius in its opposite sign, you were born with unique opportunities for self-development. But that might not be as easy as it sounds. Change in the sign of the lion, suggests that the role of the lordly male was about to be challenged. And this period was the start of men's lib, though it would take a long time to show.

Yours was the Me-first generation. Following the lead of the Boomers, you were ready to do your own thing whatever rules you had to break. Well, self-development is important, nobody can lead anyone else until they are well-centered and comfortable with themselves. But your rebellion did become a bit too selfish, which is always a danger with Leo. And using your talents for personal gain is missing the point. Uranus needs the group.

Those of you born at the tail-end of the Boomers became the yuppies, wanting the good life. Your parents experienced the ending of innocence when the remainder of the '60s brought the shocks of assassinations. Having a good time was important to them but some needed to be more open-minded. Things had to change and that meant adopting different expectations. Assuming this generation develops enjoyment in group involvement, and edges the selfish egos out of the way, the theme of "happy days are here again" could come back for communities as the century winds up. But any puffed-up dictators will have to be pushed off their perch. .

Leo provides limelight and Uranus gathers the crowds when the world is ready for new heroes. Dramatic examples of courage came in 1961 when Yuri Gagarin, was shot into space, followed by Alan Shepard a month later. But the solo performance was about to lose fame to group achievement and a different approach was taken by many successful musical groups who found new ways to perform, with electronics and outspoken lyrics.

When your generation achieved maturity, in the late '80s and '90s interest in the new age was firmly established. In your time the world will be looking for confident, well-informed leaders who have the best interests of community at heart. This combination underlies the meaning of the Age of Aquarius when

Self and society have to come to agreements about how much freedom any individual needs to fulfill his or her purpose.

On February 6, 1962, when Uranus was about to leave Leo, there was a dramatic solar eclipse in Aquarius, its own sign, with seven planets there heralding enormous changes. This produced a very talented collection of babies, known as Super-tots, who had bright minds and the discipline and confidence to be Olympic material in your chosen field. In 1999 another dramatic solar eclipse has Uranus at the same degree as Jupiter in the 1962 one forming a T-square with Mars opposing Saturn. This is a good time for these "tots" to check out their performance.

1962-68 in Virgo

Your generation has an intense need to discriminate between service and servitude so you are likely to encourage self-criticism and to be part of a change in work habits during the '90s, at your Saturn return.

Anyone who has lived in a close community knows that ego problems can get in the way of productivity. But diversity in the global village is a source of strength when individual differences are recognized. Any community requires a variety of talents to keep it strong and efficient. Adapting to the needs of a group without losing interest or confidence in oneself is the basic lesson for those of you born into this generation. It takes time for others to appreciate the quality your analytical mind is seeking. But do not give up as your strength lies in an ability to discriminate.

From the end of 1963, after the shock of John Kennedy's assassination, individuals began to wake up to their right to reject the old methods of power play. And when US forces were increased in Vietnam deep unrest was seeded about the use of military power. Society was ripe for change when you arrived and the flower children, born in the mid-40s, were disrupting tradition with their back to the land ideas and protest songs, suggesting that problems could be solved with love instead of war.

Like modern troubadours, spreading the news that something was going on under the surface, Jimi Hendrix, Bob Dillon, Janis Joplin, the Beatles and Rolling Stones brought messages that said ordinary people could make a difference. When the old structures resisted, the breaking up became more and more disruptive. Political protests grew increasingly violent as ideologies clashed.

With the birth of new political attitudes people started forming groups to share their concerns and join in mass demonstrations. Underground newspapers were sharing interest in civil rights and anti-war sentiment, encouraging readers to think for themselves.

When the rebellious energy of Uranus met the intensity of Pluto as was happening in the mid-60s, leaders attempting to make deep changes (Uranus) such as Martin Luther King, the Kennedys, and Malcolm X, were eliminated (Pluto). Beginning this new, approximately, 120-year cycle, violent social disruptions occurred before and after the conjunction, and you individualists were born, ready to clear out old ideas and substitute practical changes.

At the same time an opposing energy (Saturn) was in the opposite sign. That was a pattern of anxiety mixed with a lot of emotional tension, and led to the turning of a tide.

Your parents came in for a lot of criticism when they expressed their anti-war opinions forcefully and you may have met similar opposition in the difficult '90s when opinions were once again at boiling point. Your ideas of right and wrong do matter but it is hard to "keep the faith" when nations and countries are being torn apart over the ego of cultures and religions in Chechnya, Yugoslavia, and Bosnia for example.

An illustration of your need for patience is the changes you can make in health services, with herbs and alternative procedures. Of course you are needed, but the public has been slow to recognize you. The Virgo satisfaction comes from knowing that you are capable of doing something helpful, whether it is welcomed or not.

Uranus was at the last degree of Virgo at the time of Democratic convention in Chicago when vicious police attacks on students were viewed by the world on TV. Then came the Tet offensive, an apparent US defeat in Vietnam, wounding a powerful country's confidence that would not be healed for another 20 years, after the Gulf war. The next Chicago Democratic convention was in 1996 when the former students were in power.

1968-74 in Libra

The stay of Uranus in Libra was a half-way point in its cycle to break away from the old mold of aggression, started in 1927. The lesson now was to find new kinds of partnerships. But first old alliances needed cleaning up. With added assistance of Pluto in Libra the rates of divorce doubled in many countries. It was a signal that it was time to explore inner and outer worlds, conscious and unconscious.

A different kind of break-up was instigated by the early Boomers, who were no longer prepared to cooperate with authority. In despair, some dodged the draft by leaving the country or went off to fight a war they did not believe in. Social laws and freedoms were being challenged as never before. In some cases, young people ignited the enthusiasm of parents who were having their own mid-life crisis and were ready to work against war and the political system. You were born into a time said to have brought the worst social chaos of the century, or at least have led into it. Chaos has its positive side as it is often brings the breakdown needed to break through rigid habits that need changing.

The generations with Pluto in Leo or Uranus in Gemini were experimenting with anti-social indulgences such as smoking marijuana and changing partners. Crowds gathered at Woodstock to share new freedoms and uninhibited young people, and their children, played in the mud. Meanwhile, students were protesting in the streets of many countries, pushing past law enforcers and later, in the US, getting shot at Kent State university.

In the middle of the anti-war chaos at home, Americans added a new perspective to life, landing a man on the Moon, in 1969. Seeing pictures of Earth photographed from space was the beginning of a new relationship to our planet. This technological achievement would lead, eventually, to a partnership with an old enemy, Russia, in the '90s. This same year a supernova, called the Blue Star was sighted. The Hopi nation took this as a warning that the inner core of our planet was collapsing. The significance of that prediction would not be recognized until 1987.

An incident that showed the growing schism between government and voters happened in 1972 when clumsy political burglars broke into Watergate to subvert an election. Uranus at 29 degrees brought the resignation of President Nixon over a cover-up of information about Watergate.

1974-1982 in Scorpio

After Watergate and Vietnam were over, nothing was ever the same again. The stories of disillusioned soldiers were agonizing and John Lennon was singing "Give peace a chance." The changes brought by Uranus in Scorpio were deep and painful and took time to heal. But they were needed. Ancient knowledge was being rediscovered and new age healers were coming into their own.

A seamier side of this time was the increase in pornography and sexual abuse. The planet of change in the sign of sex was obviously going to unearth hidden opinions about who could do what to whom. Sex as power brought to the surface old battles between male and female. An obsession with freedom for the feminine side of the psyche was bringing homosexuality in men and women to the surface causing destructive behavior on all sides.

International Women's Year, 1975, coincided with a waning square of the antagonists, Saturn in the adamant sign of Leo, and Uranus in Scorpio, the battle ground of emotional power. The destructive results of sexual manipulation were being recognized as a form of slavery. Many pornographic crimes committed in this period of excessive exploitation would not come to light until the '90s, when both Uranus and Pluto had changed signs.

Scorpio is the sign of wealth and another form of slavery needing urgent solutions was economic. Big organizations were busy ranging abroad to form even bigger ones while company mergers were sending businesses into bankruptcy and throwing people out of work. Those changes were in danger of squeezing the life out of "little people" as happened in the '30s and would boomerang back in the '90s. The test for your generation, like that of Uranus in Taurus, is to ensure an equitable flow of resources so that extremes are not so destructive.

An event that would change attitudes to intimacy as drastically as the introduction of the Pill had done in the '50s, was the discovery of AIDS in 1979. That year, the outer planets were in a tight pattern with Uranus at the mid-point of Neptune and Pluto, time for new thinking about compulsive sex and escapism. It was also the year that Pluto moved closer to Earth, heightening the urge to clean up.

Heated debates over abortion, feminism and gay rights were just beginning to be of public concern. By the time this generation reaches maturity, around the first decade of the next century, perhaps these animosities can be solved.

Those who will take charge of fairer redistribution of wealth may be the generations of Uranus in Virgo and Libra. Around the end of the century gambling in casinos and the stock market had reached excessive proportions unbalancing the economic systems dangerously. There may be a lot of pain for you to clean up later, but at least it will be visible.

When Uranus was at 29 degrees of Scorpio violence was aimed at famous leaders. John Lennon, Anwar Sadat, the Pope and Ronald Reagan were all shot. Two of them survived. Prince Charles got engaged to Di, the prelude to an alliance that would upset a nation's opinion of royalty.

1982-89 in Sagittarius

During this up-beat period the spirit of independence was getting out of hand. Optimism was rampant and balloons of all kinds were going up. The cowboy image of Sagittarius recalled John Wayne as the hero on a horse opening up the west, but another kind of expansion brought an increase of terrorism and kidnapping.

The '80s have been called the decade of greed and the generation born into it will have to deal with an uncertain future. But you will be wiser about material consumption than your parents. As you are maturing, adults gambling in casinos and the stock market are throwing away their future so you will have to be adaptable about jobs and resources to safe-guard your own.

Many minds were being opened to new ideas and so were many wallets. It was "Morning in America" whatever that meant. In this period, 400 of the richest Americans tripled their wealth while homeless people were appearing on the streets. Interest rates were going up and gold reached an all-time high. After a stupid, or fraudulent, act of Congress, the Savings & Loans games were in full-swing making millions for a few dishonest people, who would not be stopped before the planet moved into Capricorn.

With its unconscious urge to reform the ego with a kind of electric-shock treatment, Uranus drops bombshells when least expected. While fortunes were being made, disasters were also in the headlines. The year of 1985 has been called the worst in the history of aviation with its crashes and hijackings. Hostages were taken in Lebanon and the knowledge of AIDS was forced on a frightened public. Among other calamities, tens of thousands of people were killed in earthquakes, mudslides, tornadoes and a ferry sinking, also there was a rash of teen suicides.

This was the year that Uranus and Pluto were semi-square (45 degrees) to each other, an aspect of warning. Also, Uranus had reached 16 Sagittarius, repeating the degree of its opposition to Pluto in their earlier cycle, back in 1901, and squaring the start of their new cycle in Virgo in 1965. Any opposition is designed to focus the limelight on what needs to be clarified and the waxing square is time for action. In Sagittarius that requires wisdom. There was an urgent need to reconsider where the urges of the two planets were taking us.

The price of independence, whether it was personal, scientific or sexual, was leading to destruction.

Another tragic example of Uranus' need to get attention came in 1986. The planet was first photographed, on January 24, then only four days later the space-shuttle Challenger exploded. Three months later came the melt-down at the Chernobyl nuclear plant in Ukraine. Unconscious reminders that scientists were not omnipotent perhaps?

In 1987 the Blue Star of the Hopi prediction was sighted again and the native people went to the United Nations to repeat their warning that if humans did not listen to the Great Spirit, destruction of the Earth was inevitable. Six months later, thousands responded to the Harmonic Convergence proving that people wanted to believe that beneficial change was possible. And in October the stock market had a temporary, though disturbing, crash.

By the end of Uranus' stay in Sagittarius, governments were being shaken up. Oliver North and colleagues were about to be put on trial for their manipulations over the Iran/contra problems. And when Saturn and Uranus met in 1988, at the end of Sagittarius, the new approach of the Soviet Union was taking effect. Gorbechev agreed to end the war in Afghanistan and gave a press conference, first for a Soviet leader, at the summit meeting with President Reagan. This change of attitude was preliminary to next year's event, when the Berlin wall came down.

1989-1996 in Capricorn

Institutions, bureaucracies and governments were due for change as Uranus went into Capricorn. After the stock market crash in 1987, employers started to downsize and reorganize, which, in the long run, could reduce waste of resources but was painful for your parents. You can grow up wiser than adults of today if you adopt a more sensible attitude to distribution and expectations by thinking of the world as one organization, with inter-related needs.

The concrete structures of government had become too entrenched and needed some bulldozers to move it. Cracks appeared when the teflon of a president from Hollywood, Ronald Reagan, began to wear thin then was broken wide open as the '80s ended with the realization that "the enemy was us," not some sinister force that required the defense of his pet project, star-wars. His massive over-spending on armaments could now be seen as extravagance that left the government coffers depleted. The public's distrust fell on his successor, George Bush, who was born into the self-deluding generation of Uranus in Pisces and Neptune in Leo. He led the country into the Gulf war on behalf of oil supplies then left to enjoy a comfortable retirement in time to make room for the next Uranus-Neptune conjunction, 1993-5. This started another 172-year cycle of changing dreams and new faith.

Boomers flocked to Washington with a young president, Bill Clinton, in 1992, ready to upset the old-ways of government. With Neptune also in Capricorn, chaos accompanied this change. The old-guard of the pre-war generations, specially any with the closed minds of Uranus in Taurus, were about to be replaced by more futuristic ones.

In the final degree of Capricorn, the Mexican peso collapsed, a situation which would lead to the ousting of the power of a corrupt presidential family and bring opportunities for a cleansed government. Also, US signed a peace agreement with Vietnam, at last!

1996-2003 in Aquarius

A wonderfully appropriate slogan of the late '90s is "the truth is out there." Interest in UFO's and crop circles had been growing for years, since Uranus in Scorpio brought out new evidence, changing attitudes to ancient beliefs but not offering satisfactory explanations. Children born now are likely to receive answers to these mysteries as your generation will have mental independence far beyond anything seen before. Astrology will be just another language and alternative medicine a natural use of common sense. By the time you can read this you will probably take telepathy and space ships for granted leaving your parents ideas far behind.

Other benefits of this widening of the mind could be international initiatives in science that will accelerate advances in education, health, communication and universal understanding.

At the beginning of the next century an interesting mutual reception (planets in each other's signs) occurs with Neptune in Aquarius, Uranus's sign, by 1998, and Uranus moving into Neptune's sign in 2003. This symbolism of a changing age from Pisces to Aquarius, with a feeling planet in a thinking sign and a thinking planet in a feeling sign, is an indication that more of us will be ready to harmonize mind and spirit.

Age of Aquarius

The relevance of the new Age, and its ruling planet Uranus, is disruption, breaking down old barriers to let the daylight in so that new growth can flourish. It promises vision and changes, but it also needs individuals to be both knowledgeable and responsible. New thinking about science and technology could release us to have more satisfying lives following an urge towards personal independence. But the downside is the impersonal domination of machines, separating us from human contact. The computer has already done that even while, ironically, it is making us more aware of the rest of the world.

As a sign, Aquarius is the intellectual which needs the warmth of Leo, its opposite. On its own it can be coldly clever with revolutionary ideas that solve problems without regard for human failings. But if it has heart, it can perform miracles of reorganization so that people can live decently, in peace, and with mutual respect.

Uranus embodies the urge for freedom that allows each person a place at the table. It recognizes the strength of difference and encourages experiments with social structures. Like a genie out of the bottle, it has been spreading its revolutionary theories around the world since it was first seen in 1781, and can never be stopped, only tamed.

Putting the love of freedom into an environment of bright mentality could bring a Shangri-La. But we have to be patient as that could take another 2,000 years.

CYCLES OF THE CENTURY

The major cycle of our time started back in 1891-92 when the two slowest planets, Pluto and Neptune came together, as they do only once in 450 to 500 years. Humanity was preparing to change from a 2,000-year lesson of the Age of Pisces to the next one, Aquarius. Since 1942 all the outer planets, from Saturn to Pluto have completed cycles with each other and begun new ones. That means that the last half of this century has been a time for new approaches to our cooperation with nature and each other, launching into a future that has yet to be molded.

As the planets move around the Sun forming angular patterns with each other like hands on a clock face, they offer a timetable to refocus the energies they symbolize so that collective knowledge can keep pace. Conjunctions of planets begin a new lesson of awareness of the effect of their urges, and their hard aspects can bring useful tests. The waxing square being a time to take action; the opposition is an opportunity for clarity; and the waning square bringing consequences. In retrospect the whole cycle shows the reality of progress in the evolution of human nature.

Neptune and Pluto — 1891-93

♇ ☌ ♆   At the end of the nineteenth century the collective unconscious was being introduced to a major transformation (Pluto) of humanity's capacity for universal love (Neptune).

Since these planets met in the sign of Gemini, communication, education and technology are bound to form the backdrop of this renaissance. On the positive side of the duo lie the intense creativity that imagination can produce (it was the era of many famous writers) and the power of investigative journalism. On the negative side though, it is a warning that words can kill and to be wary of sweet-talk and poison pens, as gossip shows its destructive power. The conjunction was specially important for the United States as it landed right on that nation's Uranus, suggesting yet another revolution, this time one of the mind and information.

It is widely assumed that until a planet is actually seen its energy remains unconscious and since Neptune was only found in 1846 and Pluto not until 1930 this new cycle was a very important step in terms of their rise into human consciousness. Their immediate warning was about war and its futility. As it is such a long cycle and its message is difficult to absorb, after two world wars "to end all wars" the mistakes have continued with Vietnam, the Gulf war and a proliferation of civil wars. The hard aspects of the cycle will not show results for another century.

When Pluto arrived on the scene the first world war had already brought a shockwave of destruction. That event exposed Neptune's illusions, sweeping away old assumptions that fighting for king and country was a heroic combat. Science with its deadly toys had brought wartime tragedy to the general public as well as the military.

Attitudes to compassion and faith, as experienced during the Piscean Age, were now being tested by Pluto so that any unhealthy beliefs could be destroyed making room for new ones to take their place. With Pluto's capacity for death and resurrection this is not an easy undertaking but it is a necessary move towards the New Age which requires less emotion and more mental involvement.

When Neptune's wish to escape is allied with obsessive Pluto many types of addictions can get out of control. The snares of Pisces, the sign ruled by Neptune, lie in the attempt to avoid reality, especially with drugs and drink, or an unconscious desire to become a victim or martyr. According to the esoteric astrology of Alice Bailey Pluto is the ruler of Pisces. That makes this conjunction even more explicit with its belief that the rays of idealism and devotion are being replaced by those of love and wisdom.

The efforts towards temperance and prohibition of the early part of the century may have been a heavy-handed way of tackling a complicated issue. When the impulse to escape accountability stems from fear surely the antidote involves understanding the problem not applying the law.

Pluto's power and obsessions require intelligent handling. Once the atom was split the old call to crusade for country, culture or religion was going to be resisted by thoughtful people who saw the possibility of total self-destruction. The misused authority, drugs and mob violence still plaguing society will have to be tamed.

Uranus and Pluto — 1963-65

A cycle lasting up to 127 years started with these slow planets in 1963-65. The Uranus' urge for independence was pushing the "edge of the envelope" (Pluto) when they met in the sign of Virgo, that area requiring analysis, discrimination and useful service. As Pluto marks the death of old ways and Uranus promotes upheavals, this is the conjunction most applicable to upsets in attitudes to employment and health. The need for new job structures and alternative medicine had to fight to the death (Pluto) the old systems. Destruction associated with Pluto can be painful but it also makes possible the transformation of otherwise moribund ideas. In this cycle the bid for freedom would meet those in control head-on. Slavery in all its form, whether to a pay cheque or a salt mine would have to change.

Those born in the mid '60s into civil unrest have seen technology, with its computers and robots, alter patterns of work. People have retired early and set up offices in their homes, while others were left without either option. The rise of unemployment and knowledge of sweat shops may be the shock needed for rethinking the effect labour, business and craftsmanship have on health. It could be a message that work needs to be satisfying as well as sustaining. To some extent we are all servants and this conjunction started new thinking about service and servitude. If life-styles could include mutual concern and volunteerism, the precious individuality a work force contains could flourish instead of being killed off with boredom.

The planets make their first square in 2012, when Pluto is in Capricorn and Uranus in Aries.

Uranus and Neptune — 1993

♅ ☌ ♆   A 172-year cycle began in 1993, when Uranus and Neptune were together in Capricorn. When revolutionary instincts (Uranus) and delusion (Neptune) get together in the karmic sign of Capricorn, this presages the break-down of traditional governance. No wonder governments are struggling with broken promises and discontented voters when we no longer trust them, or know what we want from them. This lesson could dissolve old forms of authority and demand that individuals take more responsibility for themselves.

The generation born in the years around the conjunction will experience the turmoil, and possibly the overthrow, of the "bigness" that threatens to swallow smaller organizations one by one. As Neptune represents values and the economy, mergers and manipulations of the '80s and '90s could be slowly undermined when it is in Uranus's sign, Aquarius, from 1998 until 2012.

Inevitably, the early impact of this cycle brought suspicion of governments, bureaucracies and secret dealings. It has already become a test of reputations as more sources of power have come under public scrutiny. Not all government servants, or high-flying business people, fall into the traps of corruption which often surround them. Somehow the trust in ethics and decency will have to be regained.

Apologies for past errors are being demanded of governments, often in circumstances for which they were not responsible. How much forgiveness is necessary, and how much faith we have in the renewal of honesty, will bring misunderstanding and disappointments as the cycle proceeds.

The last 2,000 years have shown the cruel side of Pisces in their aggressive orthodoxy. When faith became dominated by religious structures individuals were expected to believe what they were told without asking questions, and do what they were told if they wanted to go to heaven! Now there is a need to redefine faith. Neptune, with its mysterious power, brings the search for life's purpose, guiding human beings into its sphere of universal love. But first we have to admit that we are not totally in charge.

The shorter cycles of Saturn with these three planets add shape to the slow process of evolution. Like a frame, Saturn helps to illustrate the way their energies are being used.

Saturn and Pluto — 1914, 1947 and 1982

The two planets representing control have painful, but vital effect on the experience of generations. In Cancer in 1914, Leo in 1947 and Libra in 1982, the conjunctions were recognizable turning points in challenging and transforming the reality of over-regulation or corruption of power. They brought to light the shadow side of human nature to either tame it (Saturn) or cleanse it (Pluto).

The cycle starting in Cancer was a test of financial powers, impinging on security of family and nations. Their waxing square in 1922 called for assistance to defeated nations, but it was not given. Its opposition in 1931 showed up the depression caused by financial extremes, and at the waning square of 1940 another war, with its profits for few, was on.

Leo's cycle, of 1947, brought the baby-boomers and flower children whose self-absorption has been tested as they mature. Actions at the waxing square of 1955, from Leo to Scorpio, led to entertainment, like Elvis Presley, encouraging an increase of addiction and sexuality. By the opposition of 1965 anti-authority and civil disobedience was in full swing. At the waning square of 1973, the reality of misuse of power in Watergate and Vietnam was obvious. Those born at the start of this cycle have been severely tested as they are the new leaders able to change society.

The Libra conjunction, in 1982, started a test of willingness to cooperate. Ironically the so-called "peaceful" Libra can be very aggressive. Violence and pornography formed the environment for those born at this time. The waxing square of 1993 was anything but peaceful on all continents, with bombings, military coups and currency wars around the world. And nature provided earthquakes, volcanoes and floods in profusion. Partnerships at schools and on the streets were turning into gang warfare. Out of such horror could come the lesson of responsibility towards self and others.

The opposition of 2002, with Mars involved, could force dramatic choices between action and negotiation.

Saturn and Neptune — 1917, 1952 and 1989

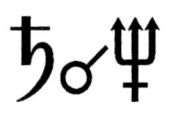

Reality and illusion were both apparent in 1917 when these planets met in Leo. WWI was no longer a time of national glory and in Russia, the lure of communism was fooling desperate mobs. By the first square, in 1926, the desire to escape reality through jazz, drugs and drink, was growing simultaneously with the desperation of starving nations. The opposition of 1936 focused on the depression caused by unbalanced economies, and the waning square of 1944 showed the failings of the strutting dictators.

A similar message of anxiety was repeated in 1952, with the conjunction in Libra, making it a cry for diplomacy and shared responsibility. This lesson of control versus confusion was nearing its waxing square in 1963, after the Cuban missile crisis. Its opposition in 1971-72, from Gemini to Sagittarius brought opportunities to share the guilt of aggression, forcing the end to Vietnam hostilities. At the waning square of 1979, from Virgo to Sagittarius, disappointments in governments and world leaders was evident.

The next cycle started in 1989 in Capricorn, where Saturn rules. Its tests were trust in traditional authorities. By the waxing square of 1999, from Aquarius to Taurus, Nature seemed to be taking action with its weird weather patterns. The integrity of biogenetics, and money markets were in question.

The opposition of 2006, from Leo to Aquarius, could echo the waning of the last cycle and the waning square of this cycle in 2016, from Sagittarius to Pisces paints another picture of the opposition of 1972. The messages keep being repeated.

Saturn and Uranus — 1942 and 1988

♄ ☌ ♅ As this 45-year cycle began at the last degree of Taurus, stability was about to meet the urge for change. A second world war was at a turning point as dictators were meeting great challenges and defining battles were fought.. The waxing square in 1952, from Cancer to Libra, was a double bid for action suggesting that Libra's sharing could offset any Cancer insecurity. But East and West were going in different directions. A post-war boom in the west was gathering momentum while Asia was still struggling. The opposition of 1965, from Virgo to Pisces, saw further mishandling of extremes as the seeds of Vietnam sprouted. The last square, in 1976, from Leo to Scorpio, was the peak of terrorism. Each of the hard aspects offered choices — to put things right, or resist.

The start of the next cycle, in Sagittarius, was a challenge to open minds so that the past made room for the future. Communism was collapsing with the Berlin wall as both planets moved into the karmic sign of Capricorn. This brought inevitable reaction to old actions before the new structures could be put in place. It was a cycle that could use dynamic tension wisely to rebuild.

The first crisis for this cycle, its waxing square in 1999 from Aquarius to Taurus, added extra stubbornness to a year already in stress from dramatic eclipses.

The opposition due in 2009 is from adaptable Virgo to Pisces and the waning square in 2021 is again in fixed signs, Aquarius to Taurus. The next cycle starts in 2032 at the last few degrees of Gemini.

MILLENNIUM

The last years of the 1990s and the first few of the 2000s hold some graphic messages. Having come through a flock of major conjunctions in the last three decades, the century ends on a dramatic note with a face-off from all four fixed signs (Taurus, Leo, Scorpio and Aquarius), closing a chapter on power and dictatorship that describe all the dangers of 1939 when Pluto moved into Leo. After Pluto presented itself, in 1930, as the atom was about to be split, the civilized world was playing Hamlet, "to be or not to be..." Possessing the means of total destruction, human nature needed to realize that all power had to be handled with extreme care. Pluto destroys in order to reseed and though its emergence from the underworld of our psyche can be painful, there are two sides to nuclear explosion — fission or fusion — blowing apart or melding together and history describes the collective choices that are being made.

This century has been cleaning out old patterns and offering a clearer view of ourselves as we step into the future. The slow planets, Uranus, Neptune and Pluto all completed long cycles with each other since the '60s and begun new ones (with the exception of the slowest pair, Neptune and Pluto, which started a 450-year cycle a hundred years ago). Uranus and Pluto were together in 1963-65, Saturn and Pluto in 1982, Saturn and Uranus in 1988, Saturn and Neptune in 1989 and Uranus and Neptune in 1993.

To understand the beginning of this finale it helps to remember the spectacular eclipse in Aquarius in 1962 when all the personal planets from the Sun through Saturn, were in the same sign challenging those universal energies. Their positions then showed a growing urge to break out of the boundaries of self-interest through three separate experiences, all causing social mayhem when they overturned the status quo, but each having positive consequences in the long run.

1962

- Uranus in Leo, liberated the Me for what seems like a selfish generation but it also taught the joy of being an individual within a group, and the strength of diversity within communities. About 1996 Pluto squaring this Uranus started the psychological earthquake that can bring out true individual purpose. In the first few years of the next century the souls born with Uranus in Leo are having their mid-life crisis, with Uranus opposite Uranus, ready to upset any life patterns that have become too selfish.
- Neptune in Scorpio was more difficult, plumbing the depths of our personal underworlds bringing unhealthy obsessions for drugs and sex to the surface, but it also released spiritual and psychic energies as well as

renewed knowledge of alternative healing. Saturn entering Taurus before the century ends, posed a challenge to rechannel emotional intensity and use the special gifts of Neptune down here on earth.

- Pluto in Virgo transformed the work place when technical knowledge started to shift power and upset patterns of employment. Computers offered easy access to data proving, or disproving, old theories and improving production and exchange of information in many diverse areas including medicine and astrology. Just as the century ends the test of Pluto square Pluto for this eclipse will decide whether to go forward or backward, to be or not to be.

A lot has changed since the '60s and where these lessons have been successful great social progress can be measured. Like a final exam, circumstances in the summer of 1999 were testing our understanding in each of the three subjects, to ensure that the difference between their positive and negative sides were obvious. Such crises come in many forms, effecting us in different ways but all with the opportunities to make progress if their challenges were accepted.

1999

The last year of the century has been a time of "high-noon" for settling scores with three waxing squares offering opportunities to take action and confront the needs and demands of communities with the resources available to meet them. These squares, all from Aquarius to Taurus, are tests of self-interest in how much must be sacrificed for the sake of our planet. The response could unmask national and international values.

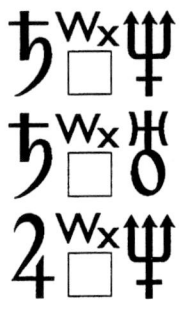

Saturn square Uranus then Neptune, and Jupiter to Neptune, all preceded the 1999 solar eclipse that tied Mars, Saturn, and Uranus into the fixed cross. That sounds like a log-jam that has to be broken, as the irresistible force meets the immovable object. Mars and Saturn had been competing in a difficult dance since January 1997, and with the solar eclipse opposing Uranus it was time they learned to cooperate, or else... Politically that can mean strong reaction to leadership and in personal life a desire to break out of what seems to be a restriction caused by someone else. For the US the opposition describes the constitutional agony brought on by stubborn attempts to overthrow a president.

In two of the waxing squares, Saturn was ready for action to construct new dreams (with Neptune) and new freedoms (with Uranus) in 1998-99, while Chiron moved into Sagittarius in 1999. At the end of the year, Chiron and Pluto, both powerful healers and/or destroyers, were together in Sagittarius, the sign of wisdom, and ready for some mass transformations.

- Saturn square Neptune tests faith. It can cause anxiety and confusion with its signal to curb any unrealistic fantasies stirred up by their 1989 conjunction. It can also build new belief systems outside traditional religions.

- Saturn square Uranus in 1999 and 2000 adds more tension. It can block the momentum of social change (Uranus in Aquarius) by limiting assets (Saturn in Taurus). The simultaneous urges to stop (Saturn) and go (Uranus) are hard on the nerves of people making big decisions. Upheavals involving physical or financial surprises have been placing new strains on governments at times of general stress, such as tornadoes, floods, or economic panic. Moving forward cautiously, avoiding over-spending while preserving collective goodwill may be a juggling act of the future needed in these conditions.
- The third square, Jupiter to Neptune, was a test of sympathy and wisdom, perhaps questioning who gets what and who cares for whom in this cosmic lottery. Trying to hold on desperately to belongings, ideas or situations, only brings pain where Neptune is concerned as its role is to sweep away whatever is no longer useful. Gaining or losing at this time can be positive opportunities. What you win you have earned and what you lose you do not need anyway, even if you think you do!

The last eclipse of the 1900s has some remarkable encores from the 1962 one. In 1962, Mars and Saturn were conjunct at 3+ Aquarius and Jupiter was 18+ Aquarius in a waxing square to Neptune. In the 1999 eclipse at 18+ Leo, Mars and Saturn oppose each other from Scorpio to Taurus while Jupiter at 4+ Taurus is again in a waxing square to Neptune, which has just fertilized at 3+ Aquarius.

That seems like a chance to assess what has been learned in the last 30 something years and channel the violence of Mars into the healing of Neptune, with the responsible discipline of Saturn. That combination could fulfill the political promises of 1989, when the Berlin wall was dismantled and foundations were being cleared for building new social structures all over the world.

Beginning this new millennium is a chance to start building on whatever foundations were laid after the convulsions of Uranus meeting Pluto in the '60s. The most recent cycle of the planet of freedom (Uranus) started in the karmic sign of Capricorn, was a high tide of change and confusion about authority. This new chapter offers opportunities for renewal, reformation, and even redemption (Neptune), if only we can understand the planetary lessons effecting our world now.

It is not surprising that so much doom was forecast by Nostradamus and Edgar Cayce if they were contemplating the outcome of the fixed crosses of 1999. Fortunately, human nature has matured since their day, or at least more people have become conscious that there are options for how we live and value ourselves, each other and our environment, and that actions, whether individual or collective, do have specific reactions.

In other words, we have more influence on the outcome than they expected. And now we are more conscious of the effect of action and reaction, the seemingly difficult energies of the slow planets can be used positively. Eclipses, oppositions, and squares can prove that though competition can be stimulating, cooperation is much more progressive. Having extreme winners and losers hurts everyone eventually and, as we are all interconnected, there is going to have to be a better balance of resources sooner or later.

The experiences of the last half-century have shaken us into new awareness and the waves of souls arriving since WWII have the mental and emotional tools to guide those born earlier through the maze of destruction and reconstruction, if they so choose. Now they are maturing and in charge, their actions and ethics will define our survival.

As the **Great Invocation** advises:
Let **Light** (Uranus) and **Love** (Neptune) and **Power** (Pluto) restore the Plan on Earth.

GLOSSARY

Chiron — a planetoid, or comet, known as the Wounded Healer, a sore point which needs repairing. First seen in 1977.	⚷
Conjunction — two or more planets close to each other, starting a new cycle.	☌
Inconjunct — 150 degrees apart, an inharmonius aspect where planets can irritate each other. Also known as a quincunx.	⚻
Jupiter — the largest planet, symbolizing the urge to expand understanding.	♃
Moon — unconscious habit patterns acquired in the search for emotional security.	☽
Neptune — the desire for perfection, often leading to confusion, escapism or guilt.	♆
Nodes — where the paths of the Sun and Moon intersect each month and yin and yang can be balanced.	☊
Opposition — 180 degrees apart, like a full moon, when two planets are facing each other on either side of the earth.	☍
Pluto — first seen in 1930, usually the most distant planet but moves closer to the earth, inside Neptune, every 250 years, most recently in 1979 until 1999.	♀︎
Retrograde — at times all planets except the Sun and Moon appear to move backward in an optical illusion caused by relative speeds of Earth and planets.	℞
Saturn — represents authority and common sense, often experienced as limitation, frustration or fear before being recognized as the karmic law.	♄
Sextile — 60 degrees apart, opportunities to work in harmony, with mental stimulation.	✳
Square — two energies 90 degrees apart, either blocking each other or producing dynamic force.	□
Trine — 120 degrees apart, providing an easy and relaxing flow of energy.	△
Uranus — planet called the "awakener" symbolizes the universal mind and mental change needed to grow.	♅
Waning — the 2nd half of a planet's journey through a cycle, past the opposition it disseminates whatever has been learned in the 1st half.	Wn
Waxing — the 1st half of a planet's cycle between a conjunction and an opposition, it is gathering experience.	Wx
Yod — when two planets, in sextile to each other, are inconjunct a third. Often called the Finger of God.	<